Bracebridge Hemyng, John Shaw

The Stockbroker's Wife

Bracebridge Hemyng, John Shaw

The Stockbroker's Wife

ISBN/EAN: 9783743318977

Manufactured in Europe, USA, Canada, Australia, Japa

Cover: Foto ©ninafisch / pixelio.de

Bracebridge Hemyng, John Shaw

The Stockbroker's Wife

THE
STOCKBROKER'S WIFE

AND

OTHER SENSATIONAL TALES

OF THE

STOCK EXCHANGE

BY

BRACEBRIDGE HEMYNG
MIDDLE TEMPLE

Author of "Called to the Bar," "On the Line," &c.

EDITED BY

JOHN SHAW
STOCKBROKER.

LONDON
JOHN AND ROBERT MAXWELL,
MILTON HOUSE, 14 AND 15, SHOE LANE, FLEET STREET,
AND
35, ST. BRIDE STREET, LUDGATE CIRCUS, E.C.
[All rights reserved.]

PREFACE.

LADIES, GENTLEMEN, BROKERS AND FRIENDS,

Most of you know I do not favour the "Cover" system. I have, however, taken a "Double Option" in this work. If there is anything bad in it, please put it down to BRACEY HEMYNG. If there is anything good, it is by

Yours faithfully,

JOHN SHAW

CONTENTS.

I. THE STOCKBROKER'S WIFE	7
II. MAGGIE'S FOLLY	39
III. CAPTAIN DAYRELL'S LUCK	71
IV. THE MISSING BROKER; OR, THE SCHEMER'S FATE	97
V. THE SPECULATING M.Ps	111
VI. THE HYPOCHONDRIAC; OR, A CURE FOR THE BLUES	129
VII. TIME AND TIDE WAIT FOR NO MAN: A TALE OF THE TAPE	157
VIII. PROMOTING A COMPANY; OR, SHRIMPS FOR THE MILLION	173
IX. THE DEFAULTER	197

THE STOCKBROKER'S WIFE.

"If Mexican Rails First Preference were 83 when stock was opened, and closed at 85¼, how do I stand with 20,000 as a bull?"

As she put this question to herself, Mrs. Langford's pretty face wore a puzzled expression. She was the younger of two sisters, and a stockbroker's wife.

"The Blessington Girls," as they were called during the short time they were out, had married remarkably well; they were each engaged before the end of their first season, Georgina, the elder by a year, securing a coronet and large fortune in the person of Lord Newberry, and Mildred Helen Maud Blessington, accepting, when only eighteen, Mr. Roland Langford, a stockbroker of high standing and great reputed wealth. This was very gratifying to their parents, who, though moving in good society, were only moderately well off, General Blessington having retired from the Army on a small pension. Two handsomer girls it would have been difficult to find in all London; and, strange to say, they had married for love, although they had money and position. Both were about the same height, but they presented a singular contrast to one another, Georgina being very fair and even fragile in appearance, Mildred, on the other hand, dark and commanding. The sisters were greatly attached to each other, and, being much alone, visited frequently at their houses, the former residing in Belgravia, the other in a large mansion in Sandown Square, Bayswater;

each kept a carriage and pair and often rode in the Park. Being a broker, Roland Langford was of necessity always in the City, and Lord Newberry was a politician and Member of Parliament, his father being the head of a ducal house, sitting in the House of Lords. It was the height of the season; his Royal Highness the Prince of Wales had that year popularised the Fisheries Exhibition, and the public were flocking in thousands to South Kensington. London was full, and the people were growing rather tired of dinner parties and balls. About three o'clock in the afternoon, Lady Newberry's carriage drove up to her sister's house in Sandown Square, in pursuance of an appointment made the previous day to go to the "Fisheries," which place they had been unable to visit since the opening, owing to their numerous engagements. Mrs. Langford, though dressed and awaiting her sister's arrival, was seated in her boudoir, a charming apartment in blue and gold, engaged in scanning an apparently hopeless maze of figures which she had elaborated on a sheet of foolscap paper. She looked very grave and perplexed as her sister entered.

"So glad you've come," she exclaimed, with an abstracted air.

"What are you doing, dear?" asked Lady Newberry.

"Calculating for a rise, love. It's all right, I think, but it does make my poor head ache awfully."

"Is there any necessity for worrying? I know the incomes of business men are uncertain. Have you met with any loss? Don't say you are going in for economy, putting the servants on board wages, selling your horses, and all that kind of thing; though I am well aware that men are mean, and make their wives endure horrors when they are pressed. Newberry refused me a cheque this morning because of some unutterable election expenses, and it is very embarrassing just now. I have to go to the Duchess of Beaumont's reception next week, and it is imperative that I should have my dress trimmed with old point."

"Point?" repeated Mildred.

"Well, I expect I shall have to fall back on Honiton or Maltese."

"I might help you if the market is favourable, and Mex. Rails go up."

"Dear me! What are they?"

"Railway stock, my dear. Roland speaks of some stocks as affectionately as if they were a child, a horse, or a pet dog. However, he has bought me twenty thousand, and I was doing a sum. You see those dreadful 'Bears' had it all their own way yesterday, but I expect things will be more favourable to-day if the Bank lowers its rate; and then again, I have an interest in St. Asaphs'; we are rigging the market with them. It is such fun."

"It is like Greek to me," said Georgina.

"Ah! but you are not a stockbroker's wife, love," replied Mildred, with an air of superiority.

"May I venture to enquire what St. Asaphs' are? Pity the density of my ignorance; I have never even heard of them. Is it a rare flower, like a pelargonium, or——"

"How can you?" interrupted her sister. "Let me tell you. First of all, do you remember Stevenson?"

"Certainly; he and Langford were paying attention to you at the same time; we used to call them the rival brokers. I thought when you refused him and accepted Roland he lost his head."

"Oh, no, that is a misconception. He flourishes like a green bay-tree, and is a great man in the House, second only to Roland, who at the present moment is, I hope, like the little busy bee, improving the shining hour.

"I never liked Stevenson," remarked Lady Newberry.

"Nor I. There is something bad in his face; ever since my marriage Roland says he has done all he can to injure him. He gets information from the 'House,' and sends strange clients to our office, and if my husband was not pretty sharp he would get bit, as he calls it. Well, you must know that Stevenson has bought up a fishing village on the South Coast, which is called 'St. Asaphs.' It is all laid out for building, and the railroad people have erected a station. At present there is only a hotel and a few bungalows, but he has got up a Company called the 'St. Asaphs' Building, Hotel, Pier, Aquarium, Winter Garden, and

Casino Company.' Here's the prospectus, read it. If not entertaining literature, it is instructive."

Lady Newberry glanced over the printed paper, informing herself that the frontage of the Winter Garden, as proposed, was to be 200 ft., width 90 ft., and it was extremely gratifying to know that it was to be constructed on the ridge and furrow principle, the building consisting of seven spans, the centre one being surmounted by an octagonal lantern, rising to a height of fifty feet. The front and one end were to consist of moulded pilasters with ornamental transom and cornice. There would be three entrances, each with a vestibule, one directly connected with the hotel by a glass corridor; a bed of plants with moulded edges would run round the building, and the temperature could always be regulated by a heating apparatus. All this and much more she could have learned, if she had been blessed with that rare virtue in one of her sex, patience, but long ere she had got to the end, she threw it down.

"Please excuse me," she exclaimed. 'Life is too short for this kind of thing,' you really must spare me the infliction; there is a limit to my endurance, dear."

"Have you grasped the principle?" enquired Mildred.

"I gather that somebody wants to build something somewhere."

"Bravo! you are improving; well, pay attention," said Mildred, with a musical laugh, adding,

"Stevenson is, as you may imagine, deeply interested in the success of the undertaking. My husband knows that he is rigging the market with them, and means to stop it."

"What do you mean by rigging the market?"

"Some clever financiers combine to raise the shares to a fictitious price. They bid against each other; the brokers act for them. The public come in and buy at a false value; the syndicate sell, and the shares go down to their true value. Do you understand?"

"No," ejaculated Lady Newberry, frankly.

Mrs. Langford shook her pretty head.

"It's very hard, dear," she replied. "I sometimes get puzzled, and I'm very sorry, but indeed I can't explain any more; all I know is we are going to give Stevenson what Roland says he won't like. But I am incorrigible. Here am I keeping you waiting, poor dear, in the most thoughtless manner; let us drop Mex. Rails and St. Asaphs', and hasten to the 'Fisheries.'"

"By all means," said Georgina, with a sigh of relief.

They were soon seated in an open landau, which rolled swiftly towards the Park, in which they took a turn, before they were deposited at the entrance to the Exhibition. Their conversation was now about trifles light as air—such as parties, people they knew, who was engaged or likely to be, who married, and who passed by in the giddy whirl of society. Then they spoke of the coming vacation, when they were going, and where they were likely to meet one another abroad in those places where fashion's votaries most do congregate. Lady Newberry forgot her trouble about the point lace, and Mrs. Langford omitted to discourse any more upon stocks and shares. Once Mildred stopped the brougham at an hotel they passed to go in and see the tapes in case there might be anything new. This made Lady Newberry very impatient.

What she had stated respecting the deadly animosity existing between her husband and Mr. Stevenson, was strictly true. Ever since she had refused him, Stevenson had shown himself the enemy of Roland Langford, but it was a secret, not an open war. When they met at dinner parties or receptions they always addressed one another in a friendly manner. Not for the world would Stevenson have allowed any one to think that he was chagrined because the beautiful Mildred Blessington had refused his advances. Yet he was a blighted being; his life was wrecked, his happiness doomed, he could not meet and look upon her without a thrill agitating his heart, and he could not conceal from himself that he still loved her better than anything in the world. He would have sacrificed wealth, honour, position, all to make her his, and it was gall and wormwood to him to think that she belonged to another. While he loved her he hated her husband, Langford feeling instinctively that the man he had to deal with was a scoundrel. In various little ways they fenced with one another, taking the buttons off their foils. "That's Stevenson's doing," Langford would say to himself as he felt the stab. "I've got to thank Langford for this," would be Stevenson's mental comment, as he owned to the smart of his enemy's thrust. Yet they shook hands, smiled a sallow smile when they came in contact, and as they were both well-known and popular, it was impossible to avoid meeting constantly. People thought Stevenson bore his disappointment very well, though they marvelled that he remained single when he could have his choice among a bevy of cultured —we were going to say " agri-cultured "—beauties. The fact was, he could not bear the sight of any woman but Mildred, and condemned himself to a life of bachelorhood for her sake. It was always a bitter-sweet for him to see and talk to her. The dulcet tones of her well-modulated voice rang like sweet bells in his ears for hours afterwards. She had once given him a photograph; he had it enlarged, and it still hung in his drawing-room. That it was hopeless to encourage a passion for her he well knew; but he did it for the simple reason that he could not help it; he had enshrined an idol, in his heart and he revelled in his idolatry. Vainly in paroxysms akin to madness had he striven to shatter the graven image; it remained unscathed after every attempt, and Stevenson was the most miserable of men. Though he appeared to be the gayest of the gay, superficial observers did not look behind the mask, or they would have seen the fumes of an unquenchable fire.

While the ladies were promenading on the terrace listening to the strains of the band they encountered several friends— for it was Wednesday, when the crowd was wont to be more select than on ordinary days—and to their surprise they saw the broker of Throgmorton Street. Mr. Stevenson had his hand in that of a young man to whom he was bidding farewell. The latter started on seeing the ladies, turned pale, and hurried away, leaving Stevenson to advance smilingly. Mildred was also astonished for reasons of her own, but she had no time to make any remark.

"This is an unexpected pleasure," exclaimed Stevenson extending his hand, and vainly endeavouring to hide a flush that rose to his face.

They shook hands with him, but Mildred's eyes followed the figure of his late companion, who was some time before he was quite obscured in the throng.

"Has business lost its charm?" asked Mildred, in her silvery accents. "Will the City survive this unusual desertion?"

"I was disgusted," replied Stevenson. "You may have heard that I am largely interested in St. Asaphs'?"

"Indeed!" answered Mildred, innocently.

"Ah! I see Langford does not bore you with details. Wise man, considerate husband, happy wife."

"Thank you. Nothing, I hope, has gone wrong?"

"There is a very considerable fall in the shares. It makes a difference of a good many thousands to me, I can tell you."

"But those things go up and down. It's a see-saw; to-day you are at the bottom, to-morrow you may be top-sawyer, you know."

"It's extremely kind of you to suggest that, but to-morrow is Settling Day, and I am likely to remain bottom-sawyer, as far as I can see. How well those foreign bandsmen play."

"Admirably, do they not? Shall you be at the opera to-night?"

"Unquestionably. It is a Patti night, I think," replied Stevenson, adding, "Lady Newberry, you look more charming than ever; have you discovered the fountain of perpetual youth and beauty?"

"Flatterer, tell me what to buy," replied her ladyship. "I want to make some money."

"You! Now you are joking."

"Yes, truly; women always want money. Those wretched farmers will not pay their rents. Do tell me what to invest in."

"Ask Langford," returned Stevenson, spitefully. "He seems to have the inside track of the market at present. Good afternoon; so pleased to have met you."

"So glad," said Lady Newberry, as he lifted his hat and passed on, after bestowing a longing look, half reproachful, half loving, on Mildred, and adding, when he was out of sight, "Horrid man! The hateful creature would not tell me anything."

"Don't you see the animus?" replied Mildred. "Roland has been 'bearing' Stevenson's market, and he does not like it. He's so wild, he does not know what to do with himself."

"Poor fellow! how uncharitable you are; perhaps you have ruined him."

"It's not so easy to do that; but he feels it, or he wouldn't have run away out of the City. He's hit, my dear, and I'm so glad. I shall have plenty of money now. What a nuisance it is they have not a tape here. These Exhibition people are only half civilised, I declare."

"All do not take such a keen interest in the City and its business as you do, my dear," replied Lady Newberry.

"I shall have a tape in my house, or a telephone. It's so nice to know how prices go. Now, if Mex. Rails are right, you shall have a couple of hundred to-morrow, Georgie."

"Can I, really?"

"Certainly. Roland never asks me what I do with my money."

"What a dear he must be. Newberry is dreadfully near. He wants an account of everything, and I do get so bothered sometimes. You know what a goose I always was at arithmetic."

"I ought to know, when I did your sums for you; but I think I can promise you the money, on the strength of what Stevenson has let out just now."

"Oh! I shall be so thankful," said Lady Newberry, wishing she had a stockbroker for a husband. "Now I can have point lace on my skirt, and plenty of it. What would you have for a foundation?"

"Don't trouble me for a moment, love," interrupted Mildred, "I'm looking for a link in a chain."

"You surely have not lost anything."

"No, no; I'm trying to think why that young man was talking to Stevenson."

"Do you know him?"

"I do. When I have been at my husband's office I have seen him frequently. He is one of the clerks; quite confidential, don't you know. His name is Sargent, and I think it wrong for him to be here with Stevenson, don't you?"

"Decidedly. It looks peculiar. I should tell Roland."

"You can depend upon it I shall, and quickly too. If it was not so late I would wire."

"You dine at seven?" remarked Lady Newberry.

"Punctually. Roland is always at home at six. To-night we dine by ourselves. It is past five now. There must be some mischief brewing between Sargent and Stevenson. They are the very last two people I should have expected to see together. He had a Judas-like look about him. I feel sure that he is betraying Roland."

"Stop it, my dear."

"If it is not too late," answered Mildred, with a thoughtful look.

"Let us go now. The crowd is getting rather mixed, and it is late, although I do not expect Newberry home from the 'House' till nearly eight; but I'll drop you at your place."

"Thanks."

During the journey, Lady Newberry said,

"Darling, do tell me what is a 'bear'?"

"He is a man who tears everything down."

"And a 'bull'?"

"Oh, he is a splendid creature who tosses everything up," replied Mildred.

Her ladyship was satisfied with the explanation, and felt quite proud of her newly-acquired knowledge.

The sisters sought their carriage, and the conversation languished as each was occupied by her own thoughts. Mildred was convinced that Sargent's interview with the Throgmorton-street broker boded no good to her husband, and she was anxious to tell him what she had seen. Georgina was dwelling upon the promise her sister had made her, and mentally laying out the money, and wishing she had a stockbroker for a husband.

"Has Mr. Langford returned?" asked Mildred of the footman who admitted her on her return to her palatial residence.

"Just arrived, ma'am," was the reply. "Master is in he library."

She entered the comfortably arranged apartment, and

found Roland Langford looking out of the window with a cigar in his mouth. His face bore a smile as he advanced and kissed her.

"Well!" she ejaculated.

"Everything firm," he exclaimed, "except St. Asaphs. I have sent them down well. Told you I would. Stevenson's so upset that he ran right away. They say no one has seen him since three. I heard that he got into a carriage on the Underground and buried his head in a paper. Never read papers myself. This age is too much press-ridden."

"What is the amount of the fall?"

"Ten per cent. and no reaction. He'll be getting up a syndicate now, and I shall go for that. Always go for syndicates."

"I saw Mr. Stevenson. Georgie called for me and we went to the 'Fisheries.'"

"Was he there?"

"Yes. And who do you think he was talking to?"

"Give it up," replied Langford. "I never could guess riddles."

"One of your clerks. Sargent, I think you call him."

Roland Langford looked puzzled, and not a little surprised.

"That is odd," he said. "I remember Sargent coming to me and asking to have half a day off, as his mother was very ill, and there was to be a consultation of doctors. That's a falsehood. Why should he meet Stevenson? He must be telling him what goes on at the office. I'll discharge him to-morrow. What did Stevenson say to you?"

"He made a casual remark about an attack on St. Asaphs' which has brought him a heavy loss, and he told Georgie you had the inside track."

"Ah! He thinks it is I. Let him. He won't get over this blow in a hurry. They call him the 'King of St. Asaphs-on-Sea,' but I'm of opinion he won't have much of a country to reign over. He is in difficulties, too, for he has borrowed money on some securities from me. By-the-way, Milly, oblige me by cutting him when you meet again. I don't like you talking to that man."

"You're not jealous of him, darling, surely?" she queried, with a soft look in her big, Juno-like eyes.

"Jealous, not I! But he was smitten with you once. Cut him."

"Very well. How are Mex. Rails?"

"They went up two-and-a-half, so I realised. Here's a cheque for you. And now my little girl can't say I don't think of her," he replied, handing her a piece of coloured paper.

Mildred looked at it in surprise.

"What!" she cried. "£500! All for me?"

"Yes; to buy bonnets."

"Oh!" ejaculated Mildred, delightedly.

The amount was more than she had expected, and giving him a squeeze of the hand and a kiss, she laughed a little laugh that did his heart good to hear, and ran upstairs to dress.

Mr. Langford had his reasons for wishing his wife to keep away from Stevenson. He feared he had some sinister design harboured in his mind against one or both of them. There was every cause on his part to hate them. If he was not working in the dark, why should he tamper with one of his clerks? Langford had been deceived in Sargent. It was not often that he was taken in, for he was a good judge of character, and during the whole of his professional career, extending over a number of years, he had only been wrong twice in his estimate of his subordinates. It was all very well to argue that Stevenson could not injure him, but he might do so. It was best to be on his guard. This last blow in the matter of the St. Asaphs-on-Sea Improvement Company could not help embittering the relations existing between them. Everyone knew that it was Langford who had helped to corner him, and Stevenson, finding himself outwitted, would very naturally be furious.

That evening Mr. and Mrs. Langford spent by themselves. They had no visitors and did not go anywhere. She played and sang to him, and he read to her. As they were about to retire, at an early hour for them, Mildred said, picking up a key on the floor,

"Why, here is the key of your safe. You have dropped it. How careless you are. Suppose you had done that in the office."

"It is the key," he replied, lighting a fresh cigar and putting some whisky in his apollinaris. "I ought to be more careful of it. I've got a lot of valuable stuff there."

"What?"

"Bonds of various kinds."

"Whose are they?"

"Oh, some belong to Stevenson. I lent him some money on a ten per cent. margin. He might at any moment redeem them."

"Does anyone know they are there?" she continued.

"Only my manager, Stratton, and that fellow, Sargent. Confound him, I'll give him the *route*, double quick, to-morrow," replied Langford, bending his brows angrily.

There was a pause, during which they were both thinking of Stevenson.

"What is my Mildred going to do with her wealth?" asked the stockbroker, looking up with a comical look.

"I'm going to lend Georgie some," she replied.

"Isn't that rather a bad investment?"

"Is it?"

"Well, I don't know, perhaps I ought not to tell secrets, but I have reason to believe that Newberry is hard up; he honoured me with a visit to-day and wanted me to negotiate some of his paper."

"Did you?" asked Mildred.

"Personally, no. I took his lordship over to a discount bank, and he was accommodated there on the usual terms. I don't lend money to relations; no, thank you."

"Does that mean that I ought not to?"

"By no means; I place no restrictions on you, Mildred, you can do as you please," responded Mr. Langford.

"Well, I shan't come to much grief over Georgie; she is very honourable, when she's got it. I mean to buy some jewellery. If she did not pay it me back, it would not worry me very much; besides, Roland, I could always ask you for another cheque."

Roland laughed at her *naïveté*, and nipped a larger piece than usual off his fresh cigar.

It may be readily imagined that Mr. Langford did not forget the supposed treachery of his clerk. He had perhaps been unwise in trusting him, but a man engaged in business cannot help placing confidence in those about him, and this is more especially the case if the business is a large one. It was only ten o'clock when Mr. Langford arrived at his office. A few early clients were in the reception room eagerly awaiting the arrival of the broker to consult him on different points, and making up their minds how to operate during the day. The clerks were all at work. Beckoning to his manager, Stratton, the broker passed into his private room. The tapes were silent; all indicated the calm which portends the rush of business which comes with the opening of the house.

"Make out a cheque for Sargent's salary," said Roland Langford, "and be good enough to tell him that his services will not be any longer required."

"We engaged him monthly," replied the manager, "at £25. May I enquire what he has done?"

"Make out the cheque for £35, and put it kindly to him, as I may be wrong. I have reason to believe that he has been giving information to the enemy in the shape of Stevenson. Mrs. Langford saw them together yesterday. There are lots of things that go on in this office that I should not care about Stevenson knowing. Besides, he told me a falsehood yesterday about his mother's illness; it is best to get rid of him."

"Shall I give him any reason?"

"Say we are reducing our staff, that is all."

"You gave him £30 to bury his mother," remarked Stratton.

"Never mind that; let that pass."

"And got his deaf and dumb sister into an institution."

"Did I? No matter."

Stratton nodded, and went away. The cheque was made out and signed, after which it was given to Sargent, who coloured slightly at receiving it, though his dismissal was not altogether unexpected by the young gentleman in question, who had for some time past been in Stevenson's pay as a spy.

"I am sorry to say that we are reducing our staff, and shall not want you any longer," said Stratton.

"You won't mind my referring to you?"

"Not at all."

"Of course you will speak well of me?" continued Sargent.

"Oh, yes; leave that to me. Good day. I wish you success," replied Stratton.

Sargent did not stay to wish any of his fellow clerks farewell. He put on his hat and overcoat as if he had been going out on business, and quitted the office, proceeding at once to that of Stevenson, who received him cordially. To say that he was furiously angry at his curt dismissal, would not be to exaggerate in the least. Although Mr. Langford had acted strictly within his right, Sargent thought himself badly treated. In his own opinion he was a victim, and he was ready to fall in with any plan suggested by Stevenson which would enable him to deal a blow at his late employer.

"You are early," said Stevenson, looking up from a pile of papers in which his correspondence clerk had marked in red ink everything that had appeared in print relative to his unfortunate St. Asaphs-on-Sea.

"I am a gentleman at large, though I feel uncommonly small," replied Sargent.

"Dismissed?"

"Yes, at a moment's notice, without any explanation. I don't half like it, though it is only what I might have anticipated when Mrs. Langford saw you and me together yesterday."

"You are speaking angrily."

"Can you wonder at it?"

"You are a little vexed."

"Langford never seemed to like me," said Sargent, thoughtfully. "He always favoured the other clerks more than he did me."

"How?"

"Oh, I don't know. I go by various things, which some would call trifles. He never offered me a cigar, he did not speak in a cheering way to me as he did to the others. I liked him once, but now I hate him."

"Really," remarked Stevenson.

"Again, he never asked me to stop after hours."

"Do you mean to say he treated you contemptuously?"

"No; he does not treat anyone contemptuously," replied Sargent. "Perhaps you can't understand me, but if I did not dislike him I should like him better than anyone else in the world. He is a gentleman, and, d—— him, I did like him."

Stevenson did not understand this feeling, but he saw that he had got something he could work upon in Sargent.

"Sit down," he exclaimed. "You want to make money, so do I. Will you help me?"

"To any extent," answered Sargent, eagerly.

"You told me yesterday that Langford is keeping my bonds in his office," continued Stevenson, restlessly toying with his pen. "Now, I want to get those bonds, for reasons of my own."

"I am sure all yours are in the safe at the office."

"Quite sure?"

"Yes; he is the only broker I know of who never rehypothecates securities deposited with him."

"I feel I can trust you as I would my own brother," said Stevenson.

"It would be odd if you could not after what has occurred."

"The fact is, I must have those bonds. The time for which I hypothecated them has nearly run out. I can't possibly redeem them, although I hoped to be able to do so."

"Why not?" queried Sargent.

"Owing to my losses. Langford's 'bearing' St. Asaphs' has crippled me."

"But if he negotiates the bonds?"

"Worse and worse," replied Stevenson.

"The markets are strong. Everyone is a 'bull' of foreign stocks. Unified are three higher than when you went to Langford. Turkish are up, and——"

"My dear fellow," cried Stevenson, with a troubled air, "I see I must put my whole confidence in you."

"Well?"

"Those bonds are stolen bonds, the proceeds of a burglary!"

At this confession Sargent indulged in a loud whistle, his face indicating the genuine surprise he felt. That Stevenson was in difficulties he knew; that he was a criminal he had not suspected.

"That's bad business," he exclaimed. "The proceeds of a robbery! Did you ever crack a crib?"

"No; let me tell you, briefly," said Stephenson. "Some months ago, a broken-down foreigner came to me with some bonds, Unified, Ottoman Banks, Turks, and others. The man's strange manner, and the value of the stock he offered me roused my suspicion. I thought he had no right to the bonds. I saw through the whole thing. My position was desperate. I determined to take them at a price, and I rang for one of my clerks. I wrote on a piece of paper the numbers of the bonds. The telephone was put in action. The answer came back: 'The bonds are stolen from the Paris Mail.' I seized the rascal by the throat, and threatening him with the police, I got the bonds at my own price. Now you see."

"But how did you deceive Langford?"

"I kept them three months, and a respectable broker like Langford never thought of questioning my honesty. Now you must help me to get them back."

"Suppose your margin had been touched?" said Sargent, aghast.

"Up to yesterday I had securities of my clients that I would have put in their place. These are used up."

"To what extent have you involved yourself?"

"About £200,000," said Stevenson, huskily. "But will you help me?" he added, impatiently.

"How can I be of use?" asked Sargent.

"You must assist me to abstract the securities from Langford's office."

"That is more easily said than done, as I am no longer on the staff."

"To-morrow is Bank holiday; if we could only get in, it might be done," mused Stevenson.

"The housekeeper does not know I am dismissed; we can get in easily enough. Opening the safe is the difficult part of the undertaking," said Sargent.

"It must be done somehow, and I will make it worth your while."

"Yes, yes; I know that you have always been very generous. Let me think; how much did Langford lend you?"

"A good many thousands. More than he would like to lose, I can tell you. I don't say it would beggar him, but he would not get over it for some time to come, if at all."

"It would be a great blow to the stockbroker's beautiful wife," remarked Sargent.

"Ah! but she is beautiful," cried Stevenson, rapturously, "and of sterling worth, too. She is as good as she is lovely."

Sargent was not interested in the good looks of Mrs. Langford, and found the subject rather tedious, so he changed the conversation, and talked glibly of the ease with which the bonds could be abstracted. It would be necessary to get the key of the safe.

"It is a Milner's safe," said Sargent.

"What difference does that make?" asked Stevenson.

"We must have the key. It cannot be picked."

"Break the lock open with a jemmy or crowbar."

"What!" laughed Sargent, "break open a Milner's safe! it is impossible. We must have the key, I tell you. I see a way to do it. Listen."

He proposed, that as he had left some private papers in his desk at Langford's he should go back for them. Stratton's desk was next to his. The key was kept in it, and during the dinner-hour he thought he could get it out. At all events he would try to do so; it should not be his fault if he failed. On the following morning all would be ready for action. Stevenson rubbed his hands gleefully as Sargent unfolded his scheme. The clerk had grasped his idea and improved upon it. Several times he declared that the thing must be done. The city on Bank holiday would be as deserted as the Great Sahara. Getting into the office by one of the numerous doors would not be difficult; an ordinary picklock would effect that, and noise would not matter. Stevenson began to see his way out of his troubles. For months the stolen bonds had laid like an incubus upon him. Every day he had feared exposure and disgrace. At each turn of the market he had hoped to make money enough to redeem them, but the utter ruin of St. Asaphs-on-Sea had robbed him of his last shred of expectation of being able to retrieve his fallen fortunes. To steal the bonds and destroy them was his only chance. He could then look Langford in the face once more without fear and trembling.

"I like your programme," said he. "Can I rely upon you to carry it out?"

"Don't you come with me?" asked Sargent.

"I'd rather stay here and wait for you. It will not require two to obtain the bonds."

Sargent shook his head.

"No," he said; "that won't do. We are in the same boat, and must sink or swim together. If I am caught you must be caught with me."

"Don't suggest such a contingency It is absurd. Who is to catch us?" replied Stevenson, biting his lips with a vexation he could not conceal. "You think I am the monkey who wants to use you as the cat's-paw to get the chestnuts out of the fire."

"Precisely," said Sargent, with imperturbable gravity.

"Well, you'll get paid for it."

"No matter. If I am to appear at the Mansion House before the Right Honourable the Lord Mayor, I want to be in good company. I should like to lean on your arm in the dock the last time I had a chance of wearing kid gloves."

"Don't try to be facetious. What good should I do you?"

"Oh, I don't know. It is not often that a stockbroker is charged with committing a burglary."

"My dear fellow, how deplorably ignorant you are of the law. It would be a felony. A burglary must be committed between the hours of eight at night and eight in the morning."

"I'm not an Old Bailey lawyer. Legal terms are nothing to me. Technical details would not help us. All I'm thinking of is that they might let me off lighter if they saw you were the prime mover in the concern. So go you must, or I shall throw the job up."

"I have an idea that as you are familiar with the place, if you were seen it would not so much matter, whereas if I were dropped upon, I could offer no excuse."

"You would not mind my arrest," replied Sargent; "it

would be fun for you to travel and think of me with my hair cut in an unfashionable manner, wearing clothes that would not fit me, and employed in some trade I was not brought up to."

"It is useful to learn a trade," said Stevenson, indulging in the ghost of a smile.

"Oh, yes, of course. When I am at liberty again I can earn an honest living, having seen the error of my ways through attending to the ministrations of the chaplain. No, thank you."

"Well, if we should fail and my presence will give you moral support ——"

"It will. Come with me, or I shall throw it up."

"You must not do that," cried Stevenson, wiping away the beads of perspiration which had gathered on his brow.

"Very well; do we work together?"

"Since you insist upon it, yes."

"That will do; I'll meet you to-morrow at one, sharp," said Sargent.

At this moment the tape began to click and roll out of the instrument.

"What's that?" asked Stevenson.

Sargent got up and looked at the tape.

"Paris prices just come over," he replied. "It's twelve o'clock."

"And my clients are waiting for me, I know," said Stevenson. "I'll attend to them presently. What does it say?"

"Markets opened flat. Rentes a franc down, Unified a quarter worse, and—what's this? Pesth and Rustchuk one per cent. better. It's a Hungarian railway, isn't it?"

"Yes, that's a joke," replied Stevenson. "Langford bought a lump of that at 67 a month ago. There are only two jobbers who deal in that stock, and they sent it down to 60. He'll have to sell at their price or keep it. Ha! ha!"

"Ha! ha!" laughed Sargent. "The jobbers know what they are about."

"Of course they do. How are Consols?"

"An eighth higher."

"I think I shall take a 'Put' of 50,000. They'll

go down before long. Yesterday there was quite an exciting scene in my office. Brighton A's had gone up; they were 104 half an hour after the commencement of business, and I will tell you what happened."

"They were very strong," said Sargent; "we had quite a fever at Langford's, everybody was buying."

"I had twenty men in the place at one time," continued Stevenson. "The majority were rich, though some were small operators and had not put up more than two cover. I never give advice as a rule, but to some I said 'sell.' Not one did. Presently we heard the tape. Click, click!"

"'103,' cried a man near the instrument.

"There was a look of blank consternation on every face.

"Click, click, again.

"'102,' exclaimed a watchful operator.

"'I'll put up another two per cent.' said one.

"'So will I, and I, and I,' cried others.

"There was a general production of cheque books, and a regular rush to write out drafts for cover.

"'Don't follow the market, gentlemen,' I observed.

"No one paid the slightest attention to me.

"Click, click, went the little monitor. Scratch, scratch, went the pens.

"102, middle price, 101, $100\frac{3}{8}$, $\frac{1}{4}$.

"The look of consternation deepened to one of blank despair. Just before that they all had a profit, but they wouldn't take profits.

"'I'll follow them,' was the cry, and I should think I took £3,000 in cheques that morning."

"How many were paid?" asked Sargent, with a sardonic grin.

"Don't ask me; the returns haven't come in yet," replied Stevenson, uneasily. "Now you are sure to be in time to-morrow?"

"I'll be as punctual as a broker on pay day."

"What do you mean?"

"He is either there or he isn't," laughed Sargent.

Stevenson smiled, and exclaimed, "I won't keep you any longer. To-morrow, at one o'clock."

"Rely upon me. I'll be here."

Shaking hands, they parted, and Stevenson was soon engaged in business, talking to his numerous clients as unconcernedly as if there was nothing whatever on his mind, and he was not contemplating a serious injury to a fellow-man who had generously befriended him in his hour of need; but no one could tell what was passing in his mind, so inpenetrable was the mask he wore.

About one o'clock he went over to the "Guildhall Tavern" to have some lunch, where he met two of his customers, Captain Beamish and Mr. Optimus Fenton, who were always in the City, and knew everything that was going on, though Beamish always had a reason for what he did, and Fenton had not. They represented distinct traits. Beamish was theoretical, and acted on the old lines. Fenton was practical. The last made money, the other did not. No one could tell why Optimus Fenton was successful; maybe it was because he went by no rule.

"Ah! here is our scrip merchant, fresh from the Rialto," exclaimed Captain Beamish. "How are my Trunks?"

"Down," answered Stevenson.

"'Alas, 'twas ever thus.' Now, I can't see why they should go down. This time last year and the year before they went up. The ice has broken in the St. Lawrence River. Trunks always used to go up when the ice broke; and besides," turning to John Shaw's work on "Highest and Lowest," "look at the quotations for the last two years."

"I sold a 'bear' of them yesterday," interrupted Optimus Fenton, who had had enough of Beamish's theories.

"Why, may I ask?"

"Blessed if I know. Because I took it into my head, I suppose."

"But you must have had some information?"

"Devil a bit."

"Ah! you are a sly operator. You won't tell," exclaimed Captain Beamish. "Information is rare nowadays though; by Jove! I remember making a pot of money years ago. The Greek Consul General and I were dining together at the Reform Club. He told me to buy Greek, as Greece was going to have a king. The stock was then 18. I 'bulled' 50,000, sir, and closed the account at 41½. Fact. Well, what do you think I did then? I called on the Consul in Pall Mall, and he told me confidentially that though the Greeks had got a king they did not mean to settle their debt, so I sold a 'bear' at 39. In short, I turned my account and got out at 23. Those were the days, sir."

"How are Brighton A's?" asked Optimus Fenton.

"Up 1."

"I bought a lot yesterday. You can realise that for me when you go back, Stevenson."

The broker nodded.

"What induced you to do that?" inquired Captain Beamish. "I do wish you'd tell me where you get your information. You are a perfect dog in the manger."

"I didn't have any, 'pon honour. The idea strikes me, that is all. By the way, Stevenson, I see your friend Langford is interested in a new undertaking."

"Indeed! What is that?"

"The West Coast of Africa Trading Association. I'm told they expect to get Lord Marshalsea as chairman. Shall you apply for any shares?"

"Not I," replied Stevenson, thinking he would not get any if he did.

"I shouldn't think that would go," said Captain Beamish. "I recollect that dismal failure, the Niger Colonisation Company. 'Shan't touch it."

He spoke snappishly, as if the association had done something to hurt him.

"I mean to have a thousand shares if my application finds favour in the sight of the directors," replied Fenton.

"Why, pray?"

"I don't know. It's my fancy."

He drank up his wine and went out.

"Really I have no patience with Fenton," cried Beamish, with a theoretical twinkle in his eye. "But I say, he must have information. What do you think?"

"I think I must be getting back to my office," replied Stevenson.

"What would you do about Trunks?"

"Sell."

"Would you really? But do you know anything? No, I

think I shall hold on, there is no ice now in the river and traffic ought——"

Stevenson did not wait to hear any more. His head was full and he could not stop to listen to Captain Beamish. It was a busy day in the City, every one was getting through all the work possible before the holidays. The Bank holiday fell on a Monday, so there would not be much done again before Wednesday. In Capel Court, as he was going into the "House," he met Langford coming out of it. His guilty conscience pricked him; he would have avoided an interview if he could, but that was impossible.

"Good day," said Langford. "When are you coming for your bonds."

"In a day or two," replied Stevenson.

"I wish you would. It does not pay me to keep my money locked up like that."

"I shall be with you in a day or two, before you expect it, perhaps."

"Mind you are."

"Don't negotiate them in the meanwhile."

"No fear," said Langford; "I'm a man of my word. I never re-hypothecate. I say, you've heard of the West Coast of Africa Trading?"

"Yes."

"If you want to secure a nimble ninepence, apply for some shares. I'll see that you get the allotment; we're sure to go to a premium."

Giving him a friendly nod, Langford hurried away, leaving Stevenson in doubt, whether he meant him well or not. The fact was Langford would do anybody a good turn, and he had no objection to Stevenson making a few round hundreds out of an undertaking with which he was connected. Why not he as well as anybody else?

Langford would fight a man in business in every way that he could, but there were many stories afloat of his kindness. An old schoolfellow came to him, shipwrecked on the sands of time, and wanted to borrow a trifle. "That would be of no use to you. I'll back a horse for you, to win the Lincoln Handicap." He did, and his friend received a cheque for two hundred pounds. He had started some people in business and had saved others from the consequences of their folly. In short, if a man fell by the roadside he was every inch the Samaritan to pick him up.

It was rather a bore to him, this West Coast of Africa company. He had been asked as a special favour by old friends to broker it and assist in its promotion. Lord Marshalsea was a great banker and a man of enormous influence in the city. His name would be a tower of strength. Marshalsea and Newberry were very intimate. He had obtained a letter of introduction to Marshalsea, who lived at Sevenoaks in Kent. Newberry had given him the introduction. He was very ready to give anything that did not cost him anything. Langford intended to go down to Sevenoaks on Bank holiday morning by an early train. It would be a disappointment to his wife, for she had planned a pic-nic in Bushey Park. They had so few holidays that they were as glad of one as a city clerk or an artizan toiling from early morn to dewy eve.

There was a peculiar charm about the old park at Hampton for both of them. It had been their trysting place in the days of their courtship. Many an hour had she wandered under the spreading chestnuts, with his arm fondly twined around her waist, with none but the graceful deer to watch the loving looks he gave her, and she had hoped to revisit the old spot on the morrow.

When he got home, Langford showed his wife the draft copy of the prospectus of the West Coast Trading, as it was already called for shortness.

"Am I interested in this, love?" asked Mildred.

"Unfortunately you are, my dear," replied he. "It is confoundedly provoking; but we had a meeting of directors to-day, and I was asked to get Lord Marshalsea as chairman."

"Newberry knows him. He will do anything for him."

"I am aware of it. I sent a telegram to Newberry, who came into the City and gave me a letter."

"Why a letter?"

"Marshalsea is laid up with the gout. It is an aristocratic complaint that runs in families. If the ball won't come to the cue, why the cue must go to the ball, and a certain hard-worked individual must go to Lord Marshalsea."

"Meaning yourself."

"Exactly."

"You promised to go out with me," said Mildred. "I was indulging in visions of sylvan shades and solitudes. How provoking. Am I never to have you to myself?"

"I think I can find a way out of the difficulty," exclaimed Langford, cheerfully. "It will not take me more than half a day to go and see Marshalsea. Suppose you drive in the brougham to Cannon Street Station and meet me there at two. We will go to Hampton, if you don't mind the holiday throng."

"I don't mind the people, but I do object to waiting at stations."

"It is not very nice."

"It is odious," said Mildred, shrugging her shoulders.

"Suppose you wait for me at the office?" cried Langford.

"That is not much better. It will be so lonely there. I will sit in the brougham outside the station. I can take a book with me, and shall not have to ornament the lounges of a waiting room, to be stared at by every one who comes in."

"Very well. Say two at the station. I'd take you down to Marshalsea's, only it would be awkward, as you don't know his people."

"Not for worlds. It would look as if I wanted to know them. I shall infinitely prefer the brougham. Don't dream I shall be lonely."

Satisfied with this arrangement they sat down to dinner, Roland Langford, by a running fire of remarks, informing his wife of what had passed during the day.

"I met Stevenson," he said, "and put him on to the new company. He looks very ill. He is coming for his bonds in a day or two. I fear there is something wrong, and can't help wondering where he is going to get the money to redeem them."

"Presumably not out of St. Asaphs-on-Sea," replied Mildred.

"They!" exclaimed Langford, contemptuously. "Since I opened fire they are scarcely worth the paper they are written on."

"Poor Stevenson! I can't help being sorry for the poor man."

"He'll never set the Thames on fire," said Langford. "I'm willing to help him, though I can't leave him alone when I get a chance of showing him that I am sharper than he is."

"That is the antagonism of business," replied Mildred.

"True, there is no friendship in business; but all the same, I don't like the man."

"You men are difficult to understand. If I so disliked a woman, and got her down, I should never help her up again."

"Yes, you would."

"Why?"

"You'd be a Christian first and a woman afterwards," rejoined Langford.

Mildred said she hoped she would if the trial ever came, but she had her doubts about it.

His promise to drive with her in the afternoon gave her something to look forward to. Even half a day with her husband was a great pleasure. She was jealous of the office because it took him away from her side. On the morrow she had expected to have him all to herself, but if she could not have the whole day the afternoon was better than nothing.

During the morning she was anxious about Roland's office. Vague fears about something that might happen there terrified her; she did not know why.

"Nobody there," she kept on repeating to herself at breakfast time.

Noticing her pre-occupation, Roland attributed it to annoyance at his going away.

"Cheer up, I shall not be long gone," he exclaimed, putting on his coat.

"Are you going?"

"Yes; I must be off, as the fly said when he got out of the mustard-pot."

This was a favourite exclamation of his. He had learnt it from an old drill-sergeant when a boy at school, and was so frequently in the habit of using it that the clerks in the office, when they saw him take down his coat, would remark, "Now for the mustard-pot."

When he had kissed her and taken his departure the sense of apprehension which had formerly oppressed her became intensified.

She ordered an early lunch, and it was a relief when Lady Newberry called to see her.

Never before had she so longed to go to the office. The nervous dread of a coming unknown evil took entire possession of her. She could neither eat with appetite or talk with spirit. She pictured the lonely, deserted office to herself; it was entirely unprotected. No one was there to watch over her husband's property, and some undefinable instinct seemed to urge her to go there at once. She had the privilege of possessing a private key. There could be no harm in calling on her way to the station. During the night she had been troubled with bad dreams—a villain had threatened her with a knife, a cat of hideous mien had sat on her chest, a huge crab had fastened itself on her back, while a number of oysters and clammy winkles were creeping slowly over her heated brow. The oysters cooled her, she felt calmed, and seized with an irresistible desire to have them shelled. She had awoke calling loudly for Chablis. In vain she tried to laugh her fears away. Go she must, and go she would.

Her sister could not help remarking her pre-occupation.

"How worried you look, dear," she said, "and how fidgety you are."

"Nobody there," muttered Mildred.

"What? Take care! you will have that glass of wine over."

"I can't help it. I fancy something is wrong at the office," answered Mildred, with an irrepressible shudder.

"What could be wrong there?"

"I cannot tell you."

"Nerves, my love," said Lady Newberry. "You should take advice."

"I shall drive straight to the office on my way to meet Roland."

"And find what? Simply the abomination of desolation of a city office on a Bank holiday."

"Very likely."

"At all events, you shall not say I detained you," exclaimed her ladyship.

Very considerately she took her leave, and Mrs. Langford hurriedly dressed herself, fully determined to carry out her resolution.

"Nobody there," was her anxious refrain. "Nobody there, and Roland away."

She recollected the look on Stevenson's face the last time she had seen him, and Langford's unwonted absence added to her alarm, and again the words came unbidden to her lips,

"Nobody there! nobody there!"

As she got into her brougham, prettily dressed in summer costume, her cheeks suffused with a flush, she looked very girlish and engaging, and any one might have been excused for falling in love with her at first sight.

Her bonnet was a triumph of the milliner's art; her gloves, of a delicate cream colour, fitted her as if they grew on her hands; her mantle of beaded silk covered her gracefully, and her small French boots just showed beneath the hem of her skirt. With the exception of being a little more developed in the bosom she was still the same fascinating girl with whom Langford had fallen in love and made his wife.

A boy with a basket of winkles on his arm paused to gaze at this rare vision of aristocratic loveliness, and the heart of the peripatetic vendor of cheap but wholesome crustacea was touched.

"She's a beauty," he cried. "When I marry that's the kind of female I'll choose."

For a moment he was a rapt worshipper at her shrine. But the stern exigencies of business recalled him to himself.

"Winkles. Tuppence a quart," he yelled, more lustily than ever, putting his hand to the side of his mouth.

There was a rustle and a shimmer of silk, the door closed, the coachman gathered up the reins.

"I'd give her a pint for nothing and lend her a pin, if I thought she'd accept of it," muttered the juvenile shell-fish merchant.

The carriage drove off, and a cook, with a red face and redder hair, came up an area.

"Winkles," she said.

The boy turned round. One look at the contrast was enough for him.

"Here y'ar," he replied, savagely; "a penny a pint, tuppence a quart; take the lot, any price you like."

Action suited Mildred. She felt better now she had started. Roland had told her to meet him at two. She did not anticipate that he would be punctual. He might be detained longer than he expected; trains run irregularly on holidays. If she was late through calling at the office it could not be helped, though perhaps it would be best to send the brougham on to the station, she thought, when she drove down Fleet Street. The city was deserted. There was not even the little life which is generally to be seen on a Sunday. Getting out of the brougham, she told the coachman to wait at the station for his master, whom he was to bring to the office, and entered. Opening the general door, she walked to the room in which she was in the habit of waiting. Beyond this again was Roland's private room, the door of which was slightly ajar.

Nobody there!

She took a seat and looked around her.

All was quiet, so painfully quiet.

No hum of voices as usual; no clicking of the tape; no hurrying to and fro of men with busy faces; no running of pens over paper; no half-deadened sound of wheels in the street without. The silence of the grave reigned in the office, as if it had been the time-honoured tomb of all the Capulets, and the stockbroker's wife felt and owned its same chilling influence.

And more than all, she missed the cheerful voice of her husband. It seemed so strange to be there alone, but she would wait a few minutes longer, and she repeated to herself, "Nobody there!"

There was nobody there after all, and a smile came to her face as she thought how foolish she had been.

One of those fogs for which London is notorious had suddenly sprung up.

It seemed to fill the room, and penetrate everywhere.

There was a candlestick on the mantelshelf, and, striking a match, she lighted it.

The fog grew denser, but no matter, in a few minutes Roland would be by her side. What excuse should she make to him for this silly indulgence in her fears? It really was very absurd, when she came to think of it. How he would laugh, in his merry, good-natured manner; she would not hear the last of it for some time to come; the temptation to make fun of her would be irresistible. She was sorry now she had stopped at the office, and wished that the brougham would return. It was not only lonely, but tedious to sit there. She tapped the floor impatiently with her sunshade, and began to feel rather bored.

Suddenly she heard a noise.

What could it be?

It sounded like a key in the second door. Was it Roland? No. What could it be? She listened intently.

Then the door opened, and two men glided into the room.

Rooted to the spot, and scarcely daring to breathe, Mildred watched them with a beating heart.

To her intense astonishment she saw that they were Stevenson and Sargent.

With her little white hands pressed together she watched and waited.

The former went to the safe and opened it with a key, exhibiting as much confidence as if it belonged to him.

Searching among its contents, he took out a bundle of papers, and, laying them on the table, cut the tape that secured them with a knife, which he put down by their side while he examined them.

"All right! all right!" he said, in a gleeful tone. "I have got the bonds, and the robbery will never be detected now."

Mildred had seen enough. It was all clear as daylight now. Stevenson, aided by Sargent, had come there to rob her husband. Her duty was plain. After all, her instincts had not misled her.

She grasped the candlestick, and, holding it up, boldly advanced.

"Help! help!" she cried at the top of her voice.

The men started, and looked in her direction.

Sargent threw the intervening door wide open.

"A woman!" he said.

"By G—! it is Mrs. Langford," exclaimed Stevenson, stepping forward and becoming pale as death.

He had advanced half way between the stockbroker's wife and the table on which lay the papers.

"Help! help!" vociferated Mildred, endeavouring to possess herself of the stolen bonds.

She was a woman of nervous temperament, afraid even to walk down a park at night, but her husband's property being in danger gave her a courage she did not think she possessed.

"The knife, Sargent! Quick, the knife!" cried Stevenson.

Sargent hesitated.

"What would you do?" he asked.

"The knife!" again cried Stevenson. "Do you hear?"

Sargent grasped it, as Stevenson made a dash forward and seized Mildred by the arm, but instead of giving him the deadly weapon he hung back irresolute.

There could not be the least doubt as to Stevenson's intention. Surprised in the commission of a crime which would make him a felon and utterly blast the remainder of his life, he was ready to go any length, even to the commission of murder. All the affection he had once entertained for Mildred was forgotten in that awful moment of panic fear.

She struggled frantically, but to no purpose.

Her piteous cries for help rang out in the corridor, but there was no one to hear them.

Stevenson continued to shout for the knife and drag her nearer to the table.

Every instant Stevenson was growing more desperate and beside himself, and at length Sargent saw that he would do Mrs. Langford a terrible injury if he did not intervene.

They were all three close together now.

Stretching out one arm Stevenson endeavoured to possess himself of the knife, but, with a quick movement, Sargent seized it, setting his teeth firmly together.

"Strike! strike!" said Stevenson, eagerly.

For a second the blade glistened in the air, and

Mildred ejaculated a short prayer as she thought her last moment had come.

"No, by heaven! you shall not murder a woman," he exclaimed, and plunged the knife deep into Stevenson's breast.

With a hoarse cry Stevenson sank to the floor, mortally wounded, while Sargent stood, with the bloodstained knife in his hand, shaking like a leaf.

"I have saved your life, ma'am, but I have killed the man," he said, speaking with difficulty.

At this moment a quick step was heard in the passage, and Roland Langford, who, finding the brougham at the station, had come on to the office, appeared in time to catch his wife as she fell forward in a fainting condition.

"Safe and unhurt! Thank God! she is safe," he said, in a voice that was deep and thrilling.

She had stopped a robbery, but she was unable to avert a tragedy.

MAGGIE'S FOLLY,

AN EPISODE IN A WOMAN'S LIFE.

MAGGIE'S FOLLY.

AN EPISODE IN A WOMAN'S LIFE.

Mr. Robert Knight, of Copthall Court, broker, age twenty-five, in possession of a good business left him by an honoured and hard-working father, and Mr. Edgar Ford Prince, called by his friends the Prince of Walbrook, where he had his offices, underwriter and member of Lloyd's, about the same age as his old Charterhouse friend Knight, were fair specimens of the rising generation of city men. They dressed in the latest style, wore stand-up all-round collars, irreproachable hats and boots, white gaiters, neat ties, handsome pins, and smoked cigarettes, affected the *Gaiety* and other haunts of burlesque, flirted desperately, but fought shy of marriage, made money quickly and spent it freely. Prince was rather effeminate, and prided himself on being what is termed a "masher," a phrase for which we have to thank the inventive genius of the word-creating American, though the philological Mr. White has not as yet given us a definition of it. Both had reason to pride themselves on their good looks, Knight being the handsomer and more manly of the two. They went into the best society, and it was said they were looking out for money. Certain it was that no poor girls found favour in their fastidious sight, though it had been noticed recently that Robert Knight had paid more than his usual meed of attention to a Miss Margaret Lindley, the daughter of a man well-known on the Wool Exchange, a very charming young lady just budding into womanhood.

It was a foggy day in November when Edgar Prince called on his friend, Arthur Knight; business was very slack, and may be described by the phrase "nothing doing."

"How-do, old chappie?" said Knight, who was standing with his back to the fire; "anything new?"

"Very little stirring," replied Prince. "I was offered an outside risk, if I liked to take it. I'm rather full, and shall have to turn it up, I think."

"What is it?"

"English-built clipper ship, 2,000 tons, bound from Philadelphia to Liverpool; name, 'Brooklyn Eagle.' Three weeks over-due since she left the Delaware River."

"Cargo?"

"Canned meats, cheeses, and corn."

"In sacks, or bulk?"

"Bulk," replied Prince.

"Ah! there's the danger; grain in bulk is apt to shift. I see they've had bad weather on the Atlantic. What's the risk?" inquired Knight.

"Owners are willing to pay sixty."

"Looks fishy, my dear boy. Tell them to keep it, though you're obliged all the same for the offer, don't you know—that's my advice. Going to the opera to-night?"

"No, I think I shall turn up at the French plays."

There was a pause, during which Prince took out a handsome cigarette-case.

"Can I offer you one?" he asked.

"Thank you. What tobacco are you smoking now?"

"Don't know exactly; these are called Russian."

"Don't touch Russians," said Knight, abstractedly.

"Eh?"

"There will be a panic in that stock."

"I'm not talking of stocks," cried Prince, smiling.

"Oh, I beg your pardon."

"These are made of Latakia, I think," Prince went on, "with just a suspicion of cut cavendish or honeydew. I always like a little cavendish. It is like Pekoe in blending tea. Oh, I say, old Lindley is going to give a ball. I've received the usual."

"So have I."

"Fine girl, his daughter; they say you are a little gone there."

"Bosh!" exclaimed Knight, adding, as if he wished to change the conversation, "I forgot to tell you that Districts are a good thing to 'bear' just now."

"Her name's Margaret; pretty name, Maggie. I once flattered myself that I was her favourite."

"You?" ejaculated Knight.

"Yes, Bob, it is a fact," answered Prince. "Don't be jealous. I never meant anything, and she knows I am not a marrying man."

Knight looked confused, and again endeavoured to turn the conversation.

"And I can advise Brums. for a fall."

"All right; I'll think of it. At present I've got my hands full of Chathams. I suppose the old man will give her a good bit?"

"Not a shilling."

"How do you know?" asked Prince, looking up in surprise.

"Told me so himself. I mean—the fact is," said Robert Knight, in some confusion, seeing that he had been betrayed into a remark he did not want to make, "I wouldn't recommend you to touch English rails at all just now. There's a big bear ring!"

"Never mind," answered Prince, "I'll admit that Miss Lindley is a very handsome girl, and we must all of us meet our fate some day. Artful dog; you've kept the secret well. When is it to come off?"

"What?"

"The marriage?"

"It hasn't gone so far as that," said Knight, colouring like a girl; "but you know I've sounded the governor, and I don't think there will be any difficulty with Maggie."

"Maggie!" cried Bob. "I suppose it's a case."

"Have you any objection to urge?"

"None whatever, my dear fellow. May you live long and die happy, is the fervent prayer of, yours truly," replied Prince. "I'm sorry, though, we shall lose you. You will be bottled up like the rest of the Benedicts. A man's not much use to his friends after he's married. Little Tottie at the 'Folly' will cry her eyes out. I never saw any woman such spoons on a man as she is on you. Poor Tots."

"She'll get over it."

"I don't know. It's my opinion she'll lose her head and marry a scene-shifter out of revenge. Have you got any of that dry cham. left?"

"No, I've knocked it off in the day-time."

"Doesn't Miss Lindley approve of it?"

"Well, she does not exactly," replied Knight, hesitatingly.

"Fond of having her own way. Ah! they all are, though she's beginning early. I say, old chappie, it's come home to you at last. You've broken a few hearts. The ghosts will rise up at the altar against you as they did to that fellow in the play, before the battle of Bosworth."

"Richard, you mean. Shakespeare's play"

"Oh, was it? I don't know. I get all my Shakespeare from Irving. Don't care to drink too deep at the Pierian spring. Interferes with business; crams a man's head up too much with useless knowledge."

"Keep all this quiet, Edgar," said Knight.

"Of course. I'm not an advertising medium. Alas! how are the mighty fallen. I have been wondering why you haven't lately dropped in at the club for a pool. Ah, well! it is sweet, I suppose, to spend one's evenings at the loved one's feet, and adore the hem of her garment."

"You're getting quite poetical."

"Enough to make me. I've received a shock. In the language of the revived P. R. I'm knocked out in the first round, and you too. By Jove! you are the last man I should have suspected of owning the tender passion and kneeling down before a woman."

"Mind your turn does not come sooner than you expect."

"Has she a sister?"

"No. Why do you ask?"

"I always cut a man when he's married, if his wife has a sister. It's dangerous. Every fellow invariably leagues with his wife to marry his best friend to a sister."

"Really."

"I've seen a dozen instances of it. It's a regular matrimonial dodge. But I say, you know, have you read *Punch's* advice to those about to marry?"

"What is it?" inquired Knight.

"It's analogous to what to do with the cold mutton: Eat it. Advice to those about to marry: Don't. By George! I'm sorry. It strikes me you'll repent it."

"Never prophesy unless you know."

"Don't be cross," added Prince; "I know I talk selfishly, and I don't want to lose you."

"You will not. You are my oldest friend. I shall always esteem you as I have done in the past," said Knight; "and I know Maggie well enough to feel sure that any friend of mine, especially so old a one as you, will be highly appreciated."

"Then it has gone so far that you are engaged?"

"I don't mind telling you—we are. It only remains for my angel to name the day. The ceremony will be very private, quite a family affair; but I shall rely on your services as best man."

"With pleasure; delighted, I'm sure."

"I don't know how it is," Knight went on, confidentially; "I worship the ground that woman treads on. I'm never happy out of her sight. It's odd for a hard man of the world like me, isn't it?"

"It is, indeed. Yet men have lost a world for a woman."

"True. Is it fate or weakness?"

"The latter. I don't believe in the rubbish of predestination. A man makes his own fate. Look at the number of fellows who come to grief through their own folly, and then howl at fate for it. It's sickening."

"I suppose you are right," said Knight. "I knew a man who went to the dogs with his eyes open, and then blamed everyone but himself for his bad luck."

"What did he do. Start a newspaper?"

"No."

"Run a theatre?"

"Wrong again. He thought he had a genius for horse-racing; bought a stud, and went on the turf without any previous experience."

"Where is he now?"

"Driving a tramcar between Moorgate Street and the North of London. I often see him, and he isn't above begging for beer and smokes."

"Some fellows have no pride in them," commented Prince. "I was acquainted with a man in the Guards who habitually broke the ten commandments, and at last got found out falling foul of the seventh. He got his head broken, had to pay heavy co-respondent's damages; left the service, and is now selling trotters in the street. I met him last week, and expressed my sympathy. He replied, with more truth than poetry, 'What is the use of your sympathy, buy a trotter.'"

"It only shows that a man should understand the business he embarks in," replied Knight.

"Yes; every one must learn a trade before he practises it."

"Except operating in stocks," said Knight. "The speculators who make the most money, in my office, are those who never came into the city before."

"Very likely."

"It's a fact. I can prove it to you."

"Not now. I really haven't time," exclaimed Prince, rising hurriedly. "Accept my best congratulations. Ta! ta! I must be off now. You wouldn't write that risk, you say?"

"No; good-bye," replied Knight, laconically.

His friend put on his hat and left him alone. The subordinate clerks had gone. There was left only old Macalpine, a hard-headed Scotchman, who had been in Knight's father's service and was now the son's manager. He always remained to the last and was invaluable, through his thorough conscientiousness and attention to duty. Robert Knight took a photograph from his desk—it was the last one Miss Lindley had had done. She was a little, fair, doll-like woman, scarcely one-and-twenty, very babyish and dainty, with small hands, feet, ears, mouth, but rather inclined to be plump. The face was not very expressive, and gave the idea of selfishness, sensuality, and deceit. This was the girl upon whom Knight had staked his future happiness. Her temper was quick and capricious, she was extravagant and fond of display, yet he could not see a fault in her.

As he had put on his coat and was about to go home to his lodgings at the West End, Macalpine entered with a card, stating that a gentleman wished to see him.

"Five o'clock; rather late to call," remarked Knight, reading on the card, "Thurlow J. Stedman, 219, West 18th Street, near Fifth Avenue, New York City."

"I don't know him, but I'll speak to him outside."

The stranger was in the outer office. He was a tall, stout, well-dressed man, apparently about thirty; face clean shaved, with the exception of a heavy, dark moustache; black hair, cut short; dark, piercing eyes, and altogether very handsome.

"I guess it's late to make a call," he exclaimed; "but you'll have to excuse me. I only reached London a couple of hours ago, and having a letter of introduction I thought I'd leave it and come down town again to-morrow."

"A letter; from whom?"

"A man you know very well. He's in business in Fulton Street; his name's Seligman."

"Oh! yes; he was a broker here. I am glad to see any friend of his. As I am going home and rather pressed for time, would you mind, Mr. Stedman, coming with me, if you are going my way?"

"I'm at the Grand, that's my hotel."

"Very well, I pass by. We can share the same cab, and I will drop you."

"I'm a thousand times obliged, that will just suit me down to the ground," answered Stedman.

They then quitted the office together.

"We will charter a hansom," continued Mr. Stedman. "I drove from the station and into the city in one of your cabs, and I like them much. They have been well called the gondolas of your streets, and they're mighty handy, too, in such a big place as London."

While they were going along towards the Embankment, the stranger explained that he had a large interest in a mine in Nevada, which he wanted to float on the English market; he would have done it in New York, but everything was bad there, and there was no confidence. Capitalists held fast; speculation was dead for a while. His friend Seligman had explained all this in his letter, and he felt sure if anyone could float the concern it was Mr. Knight, who was so well and favourably known.

"No doubt it is a good undertaking," said Knight. "Where is it situated?"

"That's just what I'm coming to," replied Stedman.

"Pardon my interruption."

"Don't say a word. The mine is situated near Virginia City, between Carson and Reno. It is called the New Comstock, and is rich in silver ore; it will be a fortune to a syndicate or to a company. I heard of it from an old miner when I was stopping at the International Hotel at Virginia City. I have worked in the mines to gain practical knowledge, and was once employed in the Virginia Consolidated, at the fifteen hundred and fifty foot level, when it was like working in a Turkish bath, the miners being naked to the waist, and working for four dollars a-day, in shifts of eight hours each. I have specimens of the ore, which is better than any in the Old Comstock lode, also deeds of conveyance of the land, and descriptive maps."

"I see you are thoroughly practical!" exclaimed Knight.

"Well, I ought to be," answered Stedman; "I'm right there all the time, I guess—you see, this thing is a Bonanza, and I'm the man who says it, and can prove what he says, Mister Knight."

"I'm glad of it, because it will simplify matters. How many ounces of silver to the ton do you expect your ore will yield?"

"I've got it all down. I want you to know it's a real good thing," he continued, "and I tell you, there's millions in it!"

Mr. Knight was prompted to ask why he brought it over here, but recollected what had been said about the stagnation in Wall Street, and refrained.

"Vanderbilt and Jay Gould have been after me," Stedman went on, "and Jim Keene was around, but they wanted too much of the plums in the pudding, and I didn't see where I came in."

"Do you know them?" asked Knight.

"Well, I should smile," replied Stedman. "Bill Vanderbilt and I are like brothers; but both of us being large operators, we don't mingle much in business. A man will lie like truth in business, Mr. Knight."

The broker had occasion to remember that remark afterwards.

"I suppose he will," he answered.

"Now, look at here—did you ever buy a horse, I ask you?"

"I certainly have."

"Well, didn't the horse-jockey try all he knew how to pull the wool over your eyes? It's just the same in our market, you can't get a square deal. There are dead beats lying in tow for you at every corner, and you are bound to get left if you don't sharpen your knife on both sides."

"We have some experience of that here," said Knight; "all flocks have their black sheep."

"Good lands! of course they have, and that's why I come to you. There's big money in the New Comstock, Mister, and I guess I wouldn't be such a mutton-headed clam as to trust the first shyster I met. No, sir, I want a man of standing, I do, and not a curbstone broker, who is working hard to go to the place where they sing twice."

"Where may that be?" asked Knight, who was much amused at the quaintness with which the American expressed himself.

"That's Sing-sing, on the Hudson River. It's our State penitentiary."

"Oh, I understand."

The cab now stopped at the hotel.

"I'm real sorry, but I'll have to leave you here," Stedman continued. "I guess it's no use asking you to dine, but I'll be pleased to have you breakfast with me to-morrow."

"With pleasure."

"I'll show you an invention of mine. We're always trying to invent something that will save labour. Mine's a patent boot cleaner. It's a box with three holes and three handles. You put the boot in the first hole, turn the handle, and all the dirt comes off; withdraw and do ditto in second, that puts the cirage on; ditto third, and your boot comes out shined up to the Queen's taste, and don't you

D

forget it. Good day. I'm glad to have made your acquaintance. I'll be expecting you at eight."

" Isn't that rather early ?"

"Not for us. We're always down town and in business at nine, but I'll make it an hour later, if you say so. What'll I order ? Beefsteak, halibut, oatmeal, some scrambled eggs, buckwheat cakes and syrup, chops and coffee ; will that do you ? Never you mind, leave it to me. I guess you won't go back on your hash. Come when you are good and ready, that settles it."

Wringing the broker's hand, Mr. Stedman got out of the cab, leaving Knight with a confused idea of things in general, for the Yankee had nearly talked him silly, as the saying is, scarcely allowing him to get a word in edgeways. After dinner at his club he called as usual on Miss Lindley, who lived with her parents at Knightsbridge. Being an only daughter, they were very solicitous for her welfare ; no objection, however, was made to Robert Knight, and she was told that she might marry him when she liked. Mr. Lindley, thinking his future son-in-law was well enough off, refused to make any settlement on her, though he promised to leave her the bulk of his fortune at his death. That evening she intimated to Robert that she would be his wife in six weeks from that date, which information made him the happiest man alive. Mr. Lindley was dozing in the dining-room. Mrs. Lindley, discreetly thinking that her presence was not required, had the good nature to retire to her bed-room to read, leaving the lovers alone in the drawing-room.

"You have made me so happy, dearest Margaret," said Robert, toying with her hand, on which the diamonds sparkled.

"Is it so *great* a thing to have poor little me all to yourself ?" she asked, in her baby way.

"You are a pearl beyond all price."

" I don't see that I am any nicer or better than other girls."

"That is owing to your modesty. I think so. You are all the world to me. I will make it the business of my life to render you happy ; you shall be my doll, my toy."

"And shall I have my own way in everything? I have been quite a spoiled child, you know, Bob."

"In everything that is right and proper, darling. I shall only exercise a husband's authority if I see you doing anything wrong, which I feel sure my little pet will never dream of."

"Will you always love me so fondly?"

"To my dying day," he said, enthusiastically.

"Shall I have the best dresses, the best horses, and the best house, and the finest jewellery?"

"As far as my means will allow."

"How delightful. I will dress to kill all the girls I know. We'll go to Paris, won't we, and get things from Worth?"

"Certainly. Paris shall be our first objective point when we start on our honeymoon."

"Won't it be nice! You must give me money to spend. I have never had much, although papa is so well off. Ma has generally bought my dresses. You won't be mean like papa, will you, dear? Not if you love me as you say you do."

"My darling shall never have cause to doubt my love. I will pour money into your lap like water."

"What a dear good boy he is," she replied, looking archly at him.

The temptation was too great to be resisted and he kissed her passionately, again and again, feeling himself in the seventh heaven of bliss. She was all his own now; but it will be noticed that during the conversation, though she had made him say repeatedly how much he loved her and what he would do for her, she had not uttered one word of love for him, her talk had been all about herself. She wanted to dress, to live in a big house, to have splendid horses, and outshine all the women she knew. Not once did she talk about his happiness, and he could not see through the thin veneer of her conceit.

The remainder of the evening was spent in arranging the details of the wedding. She would be married at St. Peter's, Eaton Square. There were to be a dozen bridesmaids, each with a little page to uphold her train, which she would have from Paris. The breakfast was to be supplied by Gunter. Everything she asked he promised her. If she had requested the Bank of England, or the London and Westminster, he would have given it her if he could. Ganem, the slave of love in the Eastern story, could not have been more the servant of passion, and all for what? a pretty doll.

Next day he was in such a good humour with himself and all the world, that he was in a mood to do all that the American stranger asked him. He did not doubt that he was a respectable man, for Seligman was not the kind of person to send any one to him with an introduction if he was not thoroughly trustworthy. Stedman was an honest looking man; but looks are not always a sure test of character. He could look you in the face and talk fairly enough. Knight was anxious to befriend him for the sake of Seligman, who had once done him a great favour, which he had not as yet had the opportunity of returning; here was his chance. This fact made him doubly civil to the American. The only objection to the New Comstock Silver Mine was that it was so far off. People are apt to look with suspicion on anything five thousand miles away, but there was plenty of surplus capital to be invested, and Knight did not doubt if he put his name to it it would succeed.

It was a beautiful day for November. The brumous atmosphere had disappeared. There had been a sharp frost in the night, and the sun shone out from a cloudless sky.

He was at the "Grand" by half-past eight, and met Mr. Stedman at the entrance smoking a cigar.

"Mornin'," said Stedman, grasping his hand; "you are on hand early."

"The sun woke me," replied Knight. "It is rather an unusual sight in November.

"Have a cigar?"

"Thank you; no. You fellows are nothing without a cigar."

"We go to bed with one in our mouth. Say, will you come to the bar? The bar-tender is a mighty good clever chap, and can fix you up a first-class A1 cocktail."

"Before breakfast!"

"It will keep out the miasma, I guess. I once had the

chills and fever when I was in Omaha, and I'm not going to give myself away in a strange country."

Against his will Knight allowed himself to be led into the American bar and have a cocktail, which was contrary to his custom, but he felt as if he could do and dare anything that day.

"Makes you feel good, eh? Don't care whether school keeps or not," laughed Stedman, seeing a smile come to his lips. "Want to let business slide, and take your girl down to Brighton Beach."

"I shouldn't mind that, for I may tell you in confidence, Mr. Stedman, I am about to be married in six weeks."

"Money?" ejaculated the Yankee.

"Well! there's plenty of money in the family, but I don't get any with the lady."

"Young or old?"

"Quite young."

"And pretty as a picture, you bet. Great Scott! what more do you want? You'll work the shekels out of the old man. He won't keep the ducats long, eh?"

He poked Mr. Knight facetiously in the ribs, making him gasp for breath.

"Don't!" he said.

"I ask your pardon. Oh, you're a long-headed one. I thought I knew something, but I guess I'll take a back seat."

"It's a love-match on both sides," exclaimed Knight, when he had recovered himself sufficiently to speak. "And I really have no designs on the old gentleman's purse."

"Well, you don't look like a man to be beaten on dollars and cents," replied Stedman, who, to change the subject, as if fearing he had made a mistake and gone too far, began to talk to the man behind the bar. "Say," he added, "haven't I seen you before up town, in Gotham?"

"Down town," was the reply.

"Where?"

"In Fulton market."

"Of course. I knew your face, but I couldn't place you for the moment. You were at Dorlan and Shaefers?"

"That was the posish," answered the barman, "but I got a recommend and crossed to this side. I recollect you, too.

Weren't you a member of the Pro-duce Exchange, and considerable on sugar at the time?"

"I was. Are you doing well in this country?"

"I can't complain, but I haven't bought a house and lot yet."

"Don't get much chance to knock down?"

"Nary chance, stranger. That's played. The game's N. G. if you tried it on. Those money-holding machines would bust you higher 'n a kite. You'd get rushed with both Bowers in your hand and be railroaded quicker nor lightning. Have another drink at my expense?"

"Don't mind if I do. Humph! What you've been tellin' me is small potatoes and very few in the hill. I should have thought you'd have been able to retire in a year, and buy a share in the concern."

"No, sirree, replied the barman, shaking his head.

"Well, I'll see your drink and go you one better; then we'll have our breakfast, for I'm getting 'bout as hungry as they make 'em at a Coney island clam-bake. Guess we'll have to count you out on this deal, Mr. Knight?"

"Yes, thank you," replied the broker, who only comprehended about half what they said.

"Set em up, Mr. Bartend, we'll have to go this hand alone."

"You're fond of playing it alone," replied the man, with a significant look, which intimated that he knew something about Mr. Stedman's antecedents, but the look passed unnoticed by Knight.

Soon afterwards the broker and his new acquaintance went into the dining room, where breakfast was soon served. During the meal, the conversation turned very naturally on the mine.

"I will do all I can to further your interest," said Knight, "and will take your scheme up for a moderate percentage."

"Now you're talking," responded Stedman. "I can see you are not easily fooled. Give me desk room in your office, and let me do the work."

"Very well, it would look better."

"Shall it be a syndicate?"

"I am more in favour of a limited company. Are you acquainted with our Companies' Acts?"

"I guess I'm not so well posted as I might be on details," replied Stedman.

"Of course a certain sum will come to you as the vendor of the property when the deeds are made over, but the liability of each shareholder is confined to the number of shares he buys and holds, and you will be expected to take a quantity in part payment. We shall have to get an influential board of directors, which will be my business."

"No one better qualified, I guess."

"I flatter myself I have a good connection."

"It will be a big boom, Mr. Knight, and you'll scoop in the dollars, sure."

"I hope we both shall. We must work for our mutual advantage and benefit."

"That's the idea, all the way. You are a thoroughbred, right up to the handle. You've got sand. I didn't know there was so much grit in a Britisher. Why we've come down to hard pan at once, and can just see how much pay dirt there is to it," said Stedman.

And so the bargain was struck. Knight was shown the plans, deeds and specifications of the New Comstock. Everything seemed regular and promising. He gave the stranger leave to nail his card to his office door, and permitted him to use a private room. In a week the company was under weigh; directors were obtained, the prospectus drawn up, and the scheme advertised. In addition to doing all this Knight introduced Stedman to his friends. He took him to see his affianced wife, who liked him. He asked him to dine with Edgar Prince, who disliked him; called him, behind his back of course, an offensive cad, and advised him to get rid of him; but Knight had gone too far to do this, nor had he the inclination to do so, for he had got used to him. Prince did not come often to the office now the American was there, and Stedman saw that he was not his friend.

"I've got myself disliked by that man Prince," thought Stedman. "He wants his friend to give me the grand shake, but he can't do it, he's too far in. I know my territory, it's all mapped out plain. I thought the suckers weren't all dead when I struck Knight, and I mean to play him for all he's worth, that's one sure thing."

Days and weeks soon passed by; the marriage took place, and the happy pair went on the continent. They were away a month. On their return, Knight bought a house at Walton, with a beautiful lawn sloping down to the river Thames, where he lived with his wife. She did not like it in the winter months because it was so dull, but he wanted her all to himself, and he had his way. It was generally twelve o'clock in the day before he reached his office, and he generally went away at two. Some days he did not appear at all. As might have been expected, his business suffered in consequence; old clients fell off, going elsewhere so as to get more attention. Macalpine and Stedman worked for him, but they could not arrest the dry rot with which the concern was attacked, and which threatened a premature decay. It was all his own fault; he was infatuated with his wife, and could not bear to have her out of his sight. So the winter rolled by with its winds and its snows and its chilling frosts, and jocund spring came with its message of glad tidings. The New Comstock Mine had been successfully launched; men and money were sent out to Nevada to develop its resources, and Stedman made hay while the sun shone, his banking account quickly going up to five figures.

"What do you think of Stedman?" he asked his wife one day.

The American was often at the house, and frequently spent Saturday to Monday there, making himself very agreeable to Mrs. Knight.

"I like him extremely," replied Mrs. Knight. "His vulgarisms are amusing. He is one of the few men who ever make me laugh."

"Then you wish him to come to the house?"

"By all means, have him here as often as you like."

Then to Stedman he said "How do you like my wife?"

"She's the nicest little quail, I guess, I ever saw in my life; too sweet for anything; good enough to eat: she's strawberries and cream. She'd knock spots out of the best of our Murray Hill beauties on a Sunday afternoon parade on Fifth Avenue, you bet."

The liking was mutual, but Robert Knight did not see anything wrong in it; perhaps he was blind—fond lovers often are. Many were the attempts Margaret made to get up to town, but Knight would not consent; he was firm in this.

"What do I want to be in town for?" he said.

"It is so dull here," she replied.

"You would be giving parties and going to them, for a lot of fellows to spoon about you, and make me so jealous that I should be fit to knock their heads off."

"Would you be jealous if men paid me attention?"

"Madly. I could not help it."

"Oh, bother this domestic life; I've nothing to do, and feel so lonely when you are away," she said, with a yawn.

"Don't say that, darling!"

"I'm buried alive!"

"Send for your mother," suggested Knight.

"She's so funny; all she would do would be to make me work at something, and I hate work!"

"Go through a course of reading—begin with Miss Braddon's novels, or the poets."

"I hate reading; you know that," she replied, yawning wider than ever, and fidgeting with the lace on her handkerchief.

"Why don't you drive out more in your pony-chaise?"

"It's a bore; the roads are always full of dirt or mud, and there is no one to look at me but a few rustics from behind a hedge."

It was evident that a pastoral life did not suit her.

"You've got Staines, Chertsey, and Egham to shop in!" he exclaimed.

"Horrid holes!" she answered.

He looked at his watch. It was a quarter to eleven. The train he went by to town would be off in a quarter of an hour, and the groom was waiting with the dog-cart to convey him to the station.

"Time to be off!" he exclaimed. "Oh, Pussy, I cannot bear leaving you!"

"I suppose men must work," she replied; "but it's an awful bore. I wish you'd been a gentleman, Bob!"

"So I am, I hope, my dear."

"You know what I mean—not a business man. Now, if

you had the time you might take me to Sandown Park to-day."

"What's going on there?"

"The races, of course; the Prince of Wales will be there, and all the swells."

"How do you know?" he demanded, sharply.

"How? Oh, I read the papers, you goose—what else have I to do when you are away?"

"I thought you said just now you hated reading?"

"Oh, I don't call that reading—what I mean by reading is hard things, like Byron and Shakespeare."

He paced the room impatiently, looked at his watch again, and then looked at the weather, which was all that could be desired, even in a capricious climate like ours. The wind was in the west, soft and mellow; the sun was warm, but not too much so; a finer day for an outing could not have been imagined, and he knew, too, that there was a good day's racing on the card.

Sandown was not many miles from where they lived. The roads were excellent, passing through an exceptionally pretty country. They would have plenty of time to get there before the Members' special arrived, even allowing Margaret an hour to dress; but on that day, at one o'clock, he had a very particular appointment. If he arranged a certain matter to his satisfaction, he would make a great deal of money—several thousand pounds, in fact; he wanted money just then. If he neglected this appointment, the business would go elsewhere. Prince had told him so, and it was a friend of Prince's he had to meet.

"Let it go," he muttered.

"What is that?" asked Margaret.

She had been watching him from under her drooping lashes, as a cat watches a mouse.

"Oh, nothing! I was thinking it is a nice day, and I should like a good game of cricket," he replied, carelessly.

"How childish you are," she said. "Upon my word, Robert, you are nothing better than a big boy."

"Say I'm your boy," he replied, with a look hungry for love.

"You know you are, you great silly thing," she answered, smiling.

He stepped forward, caught her in his arms, lifted her clean off her feet and kissed her tenderly with all the passionate devotion of a strong man helplessly in love. She was anxious to go to Sandown Park Races that day. She might have told him that she had derived her information from Stedman, who intended to be there, and would be found at a certain place at a certain time; but she scarcely deemed such an admission prudent.

"Get your things on, *anima mia!*" he exclaimed.

"What!" she cried, with a childlike laugh, "are you really going to take me?"

"Certainly, I am. Why not?"

Instantly she became grave.

"But won't it be wrong to take you away from your dear city, darling? No. I'll forego it, to-morrow will do as well, if you can spare the time; there are two days, you know, only Wales won't be there to-morrow."

"It would suit me better, yet I can see you have made up your mind for to-day."

"No, no! I won't have you making sacrifices for me like that."

"I insist upon it; be quick and dress," he urged.

The more she resisted, the more he insisted, which she knew from experience would be the case. The result was that she went up-stairs to attire herself in a very becoming costume, and he lighted a cigar, drank some champagne to keep his courage up, and sent the groom to the station with a telegraphic dispatch for Macalpine to say that he was too unwell to attend to business that day.

The drive to the course was delightful. Margaret was in high spirits; so was he. Indeed, he always took his tone from her, she was his social barometer. Many an envious glance was turned upon them as they dashed by in their well-appointed trap, and he thought he had never enjoyed himself so much.

On the course they, as he thought, accidentally ran against Stedman.

"Hullo!" cried Knight, "who the deuce would have thought of seeing you here?"

"How do? good day, Mrs. Knight—elegant weather,"

was the reply. "Why, you see, I have never been on an English race-course, and I wanted to see how one of your swell, tip-top meetings would handicap with Jerome Park. I have to see the elephant and take in the whole circus before I go back."

"And what do you think of it?"

"It's considerable of a show, and will take a lot of beating, that's a fact. I'll allow that it's some pumpkins."

"Glad that it meets with your approval. I say, will you kindly look after Mrs. Knight for a few minutes? I want to go in the ring."

"With pleasure. Must put something on, eh? That's me; I'd rather gamble than eat. Just invest a monkey for me."

"On what?"

"I'll leave it to your discretion. Shall I say you'll find me in the stand?"

"Yes, that will be the best place," replied Knight.

Giving his wife a pleasant smile, Knight, pencil and card in hand, went into the ring to back his fancy. If he had not done so he would have considered his time wasted.

Stedman conducted Mrs. Knight to the stand, and paid for two tickets, looking askance at the refreshment bar.

"I could just take a glass of wine if I was alone," he said to himself. "I had one of the English haddocks for my breakfast, and topped up with a layer of muffins, which has made me as thirsty as if I had been living on crullers and Pritzals for a week."

Margaret had no objection to being taken to a quiet corner, where they were comparatively free from observation.

"How lovely you look to-day," said Stedman, eyeing her like a satyr.

"Do you think so?"

"You're the three graces rolled into one."

"Oh! Mr. Stedman."

"I wish I'd seen you before Knight did. I'd have collared you, sure, and imported you on the other side."

"It's too late now, though I must say I should like to visit America and see Niagara, and the Yosemite Valley."

"The Yo-Semity is worth a sight of travelling to look at, you bet; good land! if you're sot on mountain scenery we can give it you. There's our Allyghanies, our Rockies, our Washoes, and our Sierras. I tell you, the old bird's got something to flap his wings and screech for."

"I suppose it's my destiny to live the humdrum life of a business man's wife," she said, with a deep-drawn sigh.

"And not much business at that."

"What do you mean?"

"Well, it mustn't go any further if I let on. Knight's as good as ruined, through neglecting his business. I've made my pile, and I'm going to ship next week."

"Going! you?"

"Yes, I ain't got no call to stop here any more, and I'm going where the woodbine twineth."

"You will see lots of pretty girls."

"You're right, the woods are full of 'em, but there's nary one that can touch one side of you, I swan," cried Stedman, with a glance of unmistakable admiration.

"Is it possible that Robert is so dreadfully involved?" she asked.

"Up to the hilt."

"Do you really mean all you say?"

"All."

"Then I shall have to give up my house, put down my carriages, sell my diamonds, and either go home to my mother or live in some dingy lodgings, and be dunned by the landlady and the tradespeople if Robert can't pay the bills."

"You've got it down fine."

"How dreadful."

He lowered his voice.

"Now I'll make you an offer," he said. "If you don't like it, don't holler. If you will come with me to the United States, you can get a divorce easy, and I'll be proud to marry you. Crossing is nothing. You shall have a first class state-room, inside berth. I'll buy you a brown stone-front house, with an English basement, and you shall lead the fashion in New York. I'll be a good man to you, and you shall have all that money can buy and all the fun you want, from a Portland cutter to go sleighing in the snow to a yacht at Long Branch or Newport in summer. If you're gone on hops, I'll take you to the Ledircranz, the Charity, the Arion, the French, to every ball of the season. I won't shut you up. You shall have your full fling. I'll even drive a coach to Pelham, to please you. Say now, will you come and join the new Democracy and swim, or stop here and sink?"

This was a queer way of making love and proposing an elopement, but it was the best he could do, and she understood him.

It was an awful moment for her.

Had she seen a pale, trembling man behind her, who was drinking in everything that was said, she might have had some pity, some remorse, for that ghost-like man was her husband. He had come back quickly. Finding them at the refreshment counter, a few words spoken by Stedman had caused him to pause. He listened; his heart was stabbed as if with a knife. Was his Margaret about to be faithless to her marriage vows? was it all true, or only a hideous dream? His brain whirled. What would her answer be to the American's infamous proposal?

It soon came.

She slipped her little hand into Stedman's, and cast down her eyes.

"I cannot bear poverty," she said; "save me, I am yours."

Horror-stricken, dumbfounded at this dreadful treachery, Robert Knight rushed away into the crowd. His brain reeled; he thought he should go mad. How bright had been his dream of bliss—it was soon over. Alas! for poor humanity, the faithlessness of woman, the treachery of trusted friends. He had lived in a fool's paradise. Staking all on the issue of a die, he had lost. He could not reproach her; his heart was too full for words; he was too much stunned and crushed even to strike Stedman and call him the names he deserved. If they had sold poison on the course, he would have bought some; if he had had a pistol he would have shot himself; but it is not always so easy to die when a man wants to. It requires preparation and opportunity to shuffle off this mortal coil, as Hamlet calls it.

He wandered he knew not whither, brokenhearted.

When close to the paddock he was slapped on the shoulder by a gentleman of middle age, who exclaimed, "Just the man I want!"

He looked up and saw Lord Packsaddle, an old school friend and a customer, who visited the shrine of Plutus occasionally, as he dabbled in stocks, as well as being the owner of a large stud of race horses.

"I'm not well," stammered Knight.

"So I should think. You don't look like a knight of old, you're the Knight of the Rueful Countenance; but will you do me a favour?"

"Of what nature?"

"Will you ride my mare, Proserpine, for the Hurdle Race which is just coming on? She's kicked her jockey, and he can't take the mount."

"Really——"

"Don't say no. You used to be able to ride anything. I know the mare's a jade, but she'll win if she's cleverly ridden. You can do it, if you like," said Lord Packsaddle.

A strange light shone in Robert Knight's eyes.

He had heard of Proserpine's reputation. She was worse than the Duke of Beaufort's Cruiser, whom Rarey tamed. Few could ride her; her temper was terrible.

Looking for death, it seemed as if Lord Packsaddle had come to him with it in his hand.

"I'll do it," he cried.

"Thanks. You're a trump! I knew you would not refuse. You must hurry up. The bell will ring directly. Come with me, and I'll give you the colours. If they don't quite fit, you mustn't mind, and I think you are just about the ticket as to weight. I'll put you on a bit at the post, and make it worth your while."

"All right."

Knight followed Lord Packsaddle to the stables like one in a dream. He scarcely knew what he was doing, but one thing shone out clearly before him like a signal lamp on a dark night. There was a chance, and not a very remote one either, of Proserpine breaking his neck.

It was soon arranged. He dressed and mounted. The

bell rang for the start and he went to the post. The field was not a large one. There were only seven runners.

A familiar face was upturned to his as he rode through the crowd.

In a moment he recognised Edgar Prince, who exclaimed, "Is it you, Bob? What next? Surely you're not going to ride that brute?"

"I am," replied Knight, with a sickly smile.

"It's certain death. She's just knocked the stuffing out of her jockey, as your American friend would say."

"Has she?"

"Don't do it; why, man alive, you must be mad."

"I believe I am a little recklessly inclined," exclaimed Knight, adding, "Edgar, do you want to do me a favour?"

"Of course; a dozen if you like."

"If anything should happen to me bury me with my mother; but that is not all, you will find Mr. Stedman with my wife."

He shivered as he pronounced the name.

"What of that? I suppose you left them together?" remarked Prince.

"Yes, I did. Now, if you got Stedman in the ring and raised the cry of 'welsher,' do you think the betting men would hurt him?"

"They'd pretty well tear him limb from limb."

"Would it be so bad as that?"

"You can bet money on it and win every time."

"Do it then," said Knight.

"Do what?"

"Say he's a 'welsher.'"

The two men looked at one another.

"You have some reason for this," exclaimed Prince; "am I not to know?"

"It is best not, as it is."

"I can guess—Mrs. Knight."

"Don't mention her name to me," interrupted Knight, fiercely.

The bell began to ring, and Proserpine pawed the ground with impatience.

"Is this your legacy of hate?" asked Prince.

"It may be my dying request," was the reply, in a voice now utterly cold and passionless.

Prince was no longer puzzled. He saw that his friend was going to risk his life, because he had discovered something he did not like and could not overlook in the relations between Stedman and his wife. Knight had always been a peculiar kind of man, never doing things like anybody else. If it had been Prince's affair, he would have thrashed the American within an inch of his life, no matter how great a scandal might have arisen, but Knight preferred to die rather than live and be dishonoured. He had done nothing, yet he felt as if all the shame was on his shoulders, and he had loved this woman so, doted on her, sacrificed everything for her, and gone to the dogs for her sake, in return for which, what had she done? treated him as a boy does an orange when he has got all the juice out of it—he was thrown away, discarded, laughed at.

"God help you and forgive you," said Prince.

"Amen," replied Knight, solemnly.

"If you come out all right you will see some fun."

Knight smiled a sickly smile, and cantered away, making no further reply. Soon afterwards the flag fell, and they were off to an even start. A sheet might have covered the lot till they got to the first flight. Then Proserpine began to show her ugly temper, and her rider was in trouble before he had gone a quarter of the course.

All at once there was a great shout.

Proserpine had bolted, and fallen at the third jump; her rider was heavily thrown and hurt, how greatly hurt was not known at first. They picked him up, and carried him on a hurdle to the stable. The crowd pressed forward to see the ghastly spectacle of a man crushed and mangled, for it was a worse accident than had at first been reported. The mare had rolled upon her rider, his neck was dislocated, and he was dead.

Though blood-stained and smeared with dirt, his face was still handsome, and there was a half-defiant, half sad expression upon it, and such a bright smile in his blue eye. Among the throng of morbid sightseers were Mr. Thurlow J. Stedman and Mrs. Knight.

"What is it?" asked Margaret.

"Some horse has thrown his jockey," replied Stedman.

"Poor fellow. Is he much hurt?"

"Gone to join the man who sat on the dynamite can, they say."

"How shocking. I wonder where Robert is?"

Suddenly her eyes fell upon the corpse, she uttered a piercing shriek, and sank on her knees.

"My husband!" she cried. "Oh God! it is my husband!"

Then her eyes closed, and she fainted away. Stedman took her up, and carried her in his arms to her carriage, where he left her after she had recovered herself, intending to see her again when he had gleaned all particulars he could of the accident.

As there were two more races on the card, he strolled into the ring. Here Prince found him ten minutes afterwards. The latter was very pale and grave. Had he not been engaged in superintending the removal of his dead friend's body he would have been after Mr. Stedman before. As it was, he was in time. Edgar Prince was acquainted with several betting men, and to them he advanced.

"The field, a pony," exclaimed one named Anderson.

"No, thank you, Andy," he replied.

"Two to one bar one," continued Anderson.

"Not to-day. I've been a J. once."

"Who's welshed you?"

"That fellow over there, smoking a cigar, with his hands in his pockets."

The betting-men crowded round him, on hearing that there was a welsher in their midst, and many an indignant glance was cast in direction of the American, who was sublimely unconscious of being an object of attention.

"I guess they don't sell any pools over here," he was saying to himself as he glanced over Dorling's correct card.

"If you say he has welshed you," exclaimed Anderson, "we'll fettle him, as the Tykes say at Doncaster."

"Do what you like to him," replied Prince.

Loud murmurs and hoarse cries arose, and the ominous words, "Welsher! hi! welsher!" sounded high above the din.

Stedman could not help hearing it, and looking up he saw that angry glances were bent in his direction.

"Those fellows look as if they wanted to put a head on me," he muttered.

Suddenly he noticed an ugly rush of men coming towards him. Clenched fists were held out, and, pale and terrified, he turned to fly. It was too late. Another party headed him off. He was between two opposing forces. Blows were rained upon him. In vain he tried to draw his pistol. They gave him no chance; they showed him no mercy.

With a desperation born of despair, he fought for his life, and by doubling hither and thither like a hunted hare he succeeded in getting out of the enclosure.

But this did not end his troubles. He was hotly pursued as he made his way towards the brougham, and overtaken ere he reached it.

"Duck him! duck him!" cried the crowd. "Welsher! welsher!"

The yells and cries seemed to arise from a thousand voices.

Mrs. Knight saw him attacked by overwhelming odds, and in a frenzy of apprehension got out, rushed forward, endeavouring to save him. At this moment one of the mob aimed a blow at him with a stick. Missing him through her intervention, he struck her on the face, laying her cheek open. The surging crowd pushed on. With a piercing shriek she fell back covered with blood. Stedman was again surrounded by the clamouring, menacing mob. His clothes were torn from his back. He was knocked down and trampled upon. This was the rough justice of the ring, and still the word "Welsher! yah! welsher!" rang out incessantly. This was sufficient to prevent any one from interfering. It was a sickening spectacle, and did not speak very well for the civilisation of the nineteenth century. Seeing how far the thing was going, Prince tried to stem the torrent. He might as well have endeavoured to stay the rushing waters of Niagara. They pushed him back and would not listen to him. He had raised a spirit that he could not lay. At length a squad of police came and bore the man away. He was alive, though fearfully beaten and disfigured. His nose was smashed. The sight of one eye

E 2

was gone. All his teeth were kicked out. Several ribs and an arm were broken. In short, when Stedman left the hospital, six months afterwards, he was a prematurely old man, and as ugly a sight as a woman would wish to turn her head away from. Edgar Prince had amply revenged his friend. Life for Stedman was worse than death.

* * * * *

And what of Margaret Knight?

She was last seen on the Boulevards, about to enter an elegant coupé.

It was thus that Prince met her near the Rue St. Honoré. He did not recognize her, and he would have passed her, but she saw him and turned scarlet under a thick Maltese lace veil she wore.

"Prince," she cried ; " so you do not know me!"

" Great heavens! it is Mrs. Knight," he replied in astonishment.

"I have not seen you since poor Robert's death," she went on. " What on earth made him ride that horse? he never told me was going to do so."

"He did not know it himself until he left you in the stand," replied Prince.

" He was not in the stand."

" You did not see him."

" Then he knew—he heard."

" Yes."

She drew her breath in quick, short gasps.

" Do you mean to tell me that he was such a fool as to go and deliberately break his neck, because Stedman said something I ought not to have listened to?" she exclaimed.

" I do."

" That was suicide."

"Precisely," said Prince. " Have you never heard of a man committing suicide because he has found the woman he loved to be worthless?"

" It is rare," she answered, shrugging her pretty shoulders. ' Fancy his loving me so, when I thought it was all an accident. I did not believe in love in this world," she added with a sigh, while a weary look came into her eyes.

" And now, Mrs. Knight," said Prince ; " may I ask you

how you could have turned against such a splendid man as your husband for a worthless scoundrel like Stedman?"

"Why? Would you really like to know?"

"Yes."

"Have you never divined it?"

"Never."

Maggie paused a moment.

"Because," she replied, "I loved you."

"You loved *me*!"

"Yes. Will you kindly assist me into my carriage?"

He did as she requested, and she raised her veil.

He shrank back with a cry of horror, for her once beautiful face was hideously scarred, so much so as to render her ugly, if not an object of abhorrence. With a reverential bow he lifted his hat.

"God forgive you, Mrs. Knight," he murmured, adding sadly, "and me too."

CAPTAIN DAYRELL'S LUCK.

CAPTAIN DAYRELL'S LUCK.

OH! fateful day.

Little did Captain Dayrell think when he started from the Waterloo Station to go to Kempton Park races that he would meet a woman who would turn his head, and give him a considerable amount of trouble before he had done with her, or, to put it more correctly, before she had done with him.

Captain Wilde Dayrell, at the age of twenty-six, was as smart an officer as could be found in command of a company in any regiment in her Most Gracious Majesty's service. He was a good looking, well dressed young gentleman, belonging to a good family, but being one of several younger sons, he had little but his pay to live upon, and was not above turning an honest penny by backing his fancy on a race-course, when occasion offered.

Sitting opposite him in the first-class carriage of the special was a man about his own age, of rather fast appearance, with a heavy watch chain, and a diamond ring on his left hand, which he kept ungloved as if desirous of showing it. His name was Arthur Roselle; his father had been a cab proprietor, and he had driven for him. When his father died he left him and his sister Rosey a good business, but he soon got rid of it, and at the time we introduce him to the reader, he had nothing but what he made by his wits. His sister and he lived together in lodgings in the Vauxhall Bridge-road, and sometimes they were in very straitened circumstances, though, on the whole, Arthur Roselle contrived, like most of his class, to live well.

It was a lovely day in early summer, and by way of opening a conversation Mr. Roselle said so.

Captain Dayrell could not deny it, and he assented.

"Do you read the papers?" asked Roselle, offering him a sporting journal.

"I never follow the papers," replied Captain Dayrell.

"Nor I. The tips of the sporting prophets are no criterion."

He liked this word "criterion," and always used it when he could drag it in, employing it with as much unction as the old lady did that pleasing one "Mesopotamia."

"Excuse me," he added, after a pause, as his companion did not seem inclined to pursue the conversation, "are you in the army?"

"I am in the service," answered Dayrell, "but I don't see what that has to do with you."

"Nothing at all. Only I was in the army myself once."

This was true, as he had enlisted in a marching regiment when he was eighteen, and been bought out of it by his father when he had been in the ranks long enough to get tired of it.

"Indeed! What regiment were you in?" inquired Captain Dayrell.

"Oh! it don't matter. I don't want to talk about it; but if you wish to know, it was the 2nd Battalion 210th Foot."

"By Jove! My regiment is the 190th, and I have been quartered with the 210th."

"That is strange. We are comrades in arms," laughed Roselle.

"Yes. Who was your Colonel?"

"Brewster."

"He is still in command. A fine old fellow I call him," said Dayrell.

"Rather a strict martinet. Are Brandon, Marshall, Owens, and Carnegie still with ours?"

"Brandon is dead; the others remain."

"Poor fellow—Brandon dead! I had a great regard for him. If ever there was a trump, he was one," replied Roselle, feelingly.

He ought to have remembered him affectionately, for Lieutenant Brandon had once, at Devonport, saved him from being tried by court martial for tampering with a comrade's kit and its contents.

"Yes," continued Dayrell, "he died in India—at Feverabad. Every one was sorry."

His opinion of his travelling companion was now a better one than that which he had at first entertained. Of course he thought he had been an officer. Roselle did not attempt to undeceive him on this point. It was not the first time he had made capital by passing himself off as an officer in the 210th Foot, and he well knew the value of being somebody if you want to get into society in England.

"Feverabad, eh!" he repeated. "I've heard of it as a deadly station, almost as fatal as Junglepore. Have you been abroad, Mr. —— ? I haven't the honour of knowing your name."

He was handed a card. On it was—"Captain Dayrell, Army and Navy Club;" and gave in exchange one with simply "Mr. Arthur Roselle" on it.

"No," he replied; "but I expect we shall be ordered on foreign service shortly."

During the remainder of the journey they became very friendly, and Captain Dayrell invited Mr. Roselle to call upon him at his club.

On reaching the course they separated; but Roselle did not lose sight of him. He watched him into the ring, and going to a booth, met a man with whom he evidently had an appointment. This was a flashily-dressed, middle-aged individual, whose red face indicated a fondness for ardent spirits. He was a disreputable person, who made bets without paying when he lost. Those who knew him called him "Daddy;" what his own name was is of no importance to us.

"Good morning," exclaimed Daddy.

"Well, it's a pretty fair one," replied Arthur.

"Can you 'five' me?" asked Daddy, anxiously.

Roselle shook his head.

"Can you 'three' me?" continued Daddy.

"No."

"By Jove! you must 'two' me."

Roselle gave him a couple of sovereigns.

"There you are. I can't bear to see a fellow hard up for a drink," he exclaimed.

"I give you my word, I'm dead broke—stony—and haven't had the price of a drink all the morning. You're a good-hearted chap, Arthur; that's a fact."

"So you say," laughed Roselle.

"I'll stick to it."

"You ought to get on, Daddy—you do try," continued Roselle, with a smile. "Now, I'm going to put something in your way."

"I'm on—like the bee on the honeysuckle," cried Daddy, eagerly.

"I'll do what I can for you. There is a young swell in the ring, about as green as grass. Make what you can out of him."

"Show me the mug, and I'll get the stuff," Daddy replied, rubbing his hands.

"Of course; come with me."

Daddy accompanied Roselle to the enclosure, and had Captain Dayrell pointed out to him. A few minutes afterwards Roselle had the satisfaction of seeing them together, book in hand. Daddy was soon engaged in pencilling some bets, and bank notes passed from the captain to him.

The day passed quickly, and Roselle did not see anything more of the captain until he went to the station, about five o'clock, to take the train home. He was very well satisfied with himself, for backers had enjoyed a good time of it, and he had pulled off some "pots" at long odds. All at once his attention was called to a gentleman, surrounded by a laughing, unsympathetic crowd. His clothes were torn, his necktie gone, his hat flattened, his face smeared with blood; and, worse than all, one eye had gone into mourning. He could have put on new clothes, but he could not alter a black eye. No one can minister to an eye diseased in such a way. Roselle recognised his friend of the 190th Foot, and pushed his way towards him. In his generally disreputable appearance he divined the handiwork of Daddy. That ingenious speculator had not been idle; he had left his mark on the gallant captain, who was furious.

"You've been in the wars. Can I help you?" asked Roselle.

"My dear fellow, I'm so glad to find somebody I know," replied Captain Dayrell. "You can buy me a ticket back to London."

"Have you lost your return?"

"I've lost everything; I fell among thieves. The man I bet with robbed me, and when I asked for my money which I had won, he and some roughs knocked me about, and cleared me out."

Arthur Roselle shook his head.

"You cannot be too careful to whom you speak in places like this," he said. "Stay here; I'll be back in a moment."

He turned away to hide a smile, and, purchasing a ticket, helped his friend into a carriage, taking a seat by his side. The train moved out of the station directly afterwards, and they resumed the conversation. Daddy had done his work thoroughly, as was his custom, for the wretched victim was penniless. Of twenty-five pounds with which he had started in the morning, not a shilling was left him. Daddy was a sure card for Roselle to play. He never failed.

"What on earth am I to do about my eye? it is nearly closed, and I am sure it is as black as night," remarked Dayrell.

"It is a bad eye," replied Roselle. "How long does your leave last?"

"Ten days; but I can get it extended."

"Where are you quartered?"

"At Shorncliffe."

"I can get you a bedroom in my house," remarked Roselle. "If you like to hide away there for a few days, until you can pass muster, you are welcome. My sister and I will look after you."

"How kind. I accept your offer at once," answered Dayrell, eagerly.

"We will get out at Vauxhall. I live close by."

"Many thanks. I must go into quarantine, and with some books, some beef, and some beer, life will be endurable."

"We will try to make it so for you."

"I shall be everlastingly obliged to you. Confound that scoundrel who 'welshed' me."

"Ha! ha! it is rather a good joke. What was he like?"

"Tall and thin, with an eye like a hawk. Do you know him? but how should you."

"No; I am happy to say I do not," replied Roselle, with unblushing effrontery; "I only go to race-courses for amusement, and seldom make a bet. Since I was invalided out of the service a relation kindly died, and left my sister and me enough to live upon."

"Oh! you were invalided?"

"Didn't I tell you so? Fact is, I went the pace rather too much at first, and broke down."

"And you have a sister?"

"One. Her name is Rosey. She is a very good girl, but if she cooks the forequarter of lamb I ordered for dinner too much I shall have to scold her."

"Does she cook?"

"She does not belong to the ornamental division, though the girl is fairly educated. She neither sings nor plays. She can't talk French, and never did a stitch of crewel work. I doubt if she could show you Madagascar on the map, or tell you if an elephant is graminivorous or carnivorous; but I'll back her to sew on buttons, and send up a dinner against any one you like to nominate."

"What a relief."

"Why?"

"It will be refreshing to meet a girl of that sort in these days of cramming and high pressure. Every petty tradesman's daughter is over educated now; but what will she say to my eye?" asked the captain, nervously.

"She's seen me with a worse one, and will probably apply raw beef."

"What an invaluable girl."

"You'll say so when you know her," answered Roselle.

Captain Dayrell began to get quite interested in this sister, and if he had not thought it rude he would have inquired what height, size, and colour she was. In fact

Rosey Roselle was a handsome woman, between nineteen and twenty. She was tall and well formed, with large liquid black eyes, and a wealth of raven tresses, which she tied in a knot behind, and wore frizzed over her forehead. She had not as yet fallen in love with any one, though she walked out on Sunday with a friend of her brother's, named Tom Nash, who was a billiard-marker at a neighbouring tavern, and about as despicable a little cad as could be met with in a day's march. He was very fond of Rosey, but though she had the bad taste to like him, she had not irrevocably given him her affection.

Such was the state of affairs when Captain Dayrell was brought to the house in which they lodged. The Roselles' apartments consisted of two bedrooms, a sitting room, and a kitchen, Rosey being in the latter when they ascended the stairs to the first floor.

"Is that you, Arthur?" asked Miss Roselle.

"Yes, my dear, and I have brought a friend home to dinner."

"Then I wish you wouldn't without telling me. We don't keep an hotel. This lamb's nearly done, and I haven't got enough mint for the sauce. You'll have to go and buy a penn'orth, and you may as well get the beer at the same time. What luck did you have at Kempton?"

Arthur Roselle pushed his new friend forward to the door of the kitchen, which was at the head of the stairs.

"Captain Dayrell, my dear," he said; "I'll leave you to do the honours while I go and execute your commissions."

Saying this, he left them together. Rosey was very blunt and outspoken. She was veritably a child of nature, who did not stand upon ceremony.

Directly she saw Captain Dayrell she threw up her hands, and burst out laughing.

"What a shame," she cried; "you've had your head hammered."

"I am sorry to confess, Miss Roselle, that I have undergone that painful operation,' replied Dayrell.

"It will take you a week to mend that eye," she continued, reflectively. 'You'd better put a piece of steak on it. That's what I do for Arthur. Run and buy half a pound. There's a butcher's shop round the corner. Have you got any money?"

Captain Dayrell shook his head.

"Ah! they saw you coming, of course," she said, enigmatically. "Here's a shilling for you; make haste. You can't go about with an eye like that."

The captain took the money with a smile, and went to the butcher's shop, as she had directed him. She was evidently accustomed to having her own way, and it would have been useless to refuse her. He looked neither to the right nor to the left. When he came back, Miss Roselle considerately tied the application over his eye, with a handkerchief, and gave him a chair in the parlour.

"You'll do," she exclaimed. "I can't stop to talk to you now, or the dinner will be spoiled. Having put the meat on your eye, I must eye your meat."

She was gone like a thought, and Captain Dayrell was at liberty to survey his surroundings with one eye, and indulge his reflections.

"What a fine creature," he muttered. "But what a rough diamond. She wants a lot of training before she'd win the Drawing Room Stakes."

There is a spice of the Bohemian in all of us. Dayrell felt pleased to escape for a time from the precision of military life, and the surroundings of fashionable society. When Roselle came back, and the dinner was placed upon the table, he enjoyed it as much as he would have done turtle and venison, salmon and game, at the regimental mess, and the beer from "round the corner" was as good as any champagne. To wind up with there was cheese and salad.

Arthur having brought in some Gruyère, Roscy offered it to Captain Dayrell, saying, "Will you take some 'Grew Here?'"

He had a good mind to reply that he would rather have some that didn't "Grow There;" but he refrained, and helped himself.

This was a solecism, but he did not like her any the less for it.

Seeing that he had to be the guest of the Roselles for

some time, whether he liked it or not, he determined to make himself thoroughly at home. Arthur talked well, and showed that he was a thorough man of the world, though his morality was not of a high standard. While the men smoked, and drank whisky with soda, Rosey sat on a sofa sewing. Though she did not appear to take much notice of the young captain, she constantly glanced furtively in his direction, and owned to herself that he was handsome. He was a thoroughbred gentleman, too, which always goes a great way with girls of her class.

"How do you find yourself by this time?" asked Arthur Roselle, when the curtains were drawn, and the lamp lighted.

"My throat is sore; in the scuffle it must have been squeezed," replied Dayrell.

"Try a *belladonna*."

"What's that?"

Roselle took a little box from his pocket, containing globules of the homœopathic school, and offered it to him.

"If that don't do you any good, I can offer you a *nux vomica*," he said; and seeing that the captain hesitated, he added, "Don't be afraid; they are like our English guns in the Soudan—there's no danger in them."

Dayrell laughed, and took a pill.

"I always take my medicine as I pay my debts, in homœopathic doses," Arthur went on. "Heigho! I wish I had some snug berth, say that of a County Court Judge."

"Oh, yes! and adjudicate on your own cases," answered Dayrell.

"Come, that's too bad," remonstrated Roselle.

"Why not wish for a private gold mine?"

"Wealth, my dear fellow, is a fraud," replied Roselle, sententiously. "I am young and strong, and can always make money. I repeat, wealth is a fraud. What you want is the capacity for enjoying it. If you can't enjoy it, what is the good of it? I tell you it is like salmon without the lobster sauce."

"You are in the right," answered Dayrell, reflectively.

"Fancy a big fish like the salmon founding its reputation on a little fish like the lobster," Roselle continued.

F

"It seems to me, that we waste our time in either reflecting on the past or anticipating the future."

"What ought we to do, then?" asked Roselle, who did not quite catch his drift.

"Why, enjoy the present, of course," replied Captain Dayrell, taking a sly glance at Rosey.

They lighted fresh cigars.

"You say you make money," continued Dayrell.

"Yes, two months ago I netted a cool thou. on the Stock Exchange, and Rosey and I went to Paris and spent it; didn't we, Rosey?"

"It didn't take you long to spend it," answered Rosey.

"Come! you had your share of the enjoyment."

"I'm not saying I didn't, but I'd rather have had a couple of new dresses."

"There's ingratitude for you, Mr. Dayrell," cried Roselle.

"I think your sister would pay for dress," said Dayrell.

Rosey thanked him with a look for this speech.

"Let her wait till she gets a husband. I'm not going to dress her," answered Roselle, in a tone which Dayrell thought rather unkind.

"Wait till I ask you," replied Rosey, sharply.

The captain, thinking there might be a quarrel, took up the parable of wealth, and exclaimed, "Tell me something about stocks."

"With pleasure," said Roselle. "I must tell you that I am a great speculator. I'd buy anything, if I thought I could make money out of it, from Egyptian Unified to a dead donkey. I only go to races for the fun and excitement of the thing. When I made the thou. I was telling you about, I was a 'bull' of New York Centrals. My brokers are Messrs. Hard and Fast, of Cornhill. I'll introduce you, if you like."

"But I know nothing about the business."

"I'll soon tell you. Last week I was within an ace of pulling off a good thing. I was a 'bear' of Districts, and had opened up £2,000 stock with a 2 per cent. cover. Prices kept coming in. It was up 1 per cent. I began to feel uncomfortable, for the £20 cover I had put up was all the money I had with me, and Hard and Fast are very particular men. The tape was at work again. It was 2 up. The limit was touched. My cover was gone."

"'I'll put up fresh cover,' I said to Hard and Fast, both of whom were standing near me.

"'Closed,' was the reply.

"'Don't say that! You will have some mercy on me,' I cried.

"'It's no use; the account's closed.'

"A few minutes afterwards the reaction I had expected came, and the stock went down 4 in one day."

"How very annoying," remarked Captain Dayrell. "I wish you would explain to me how it is done."

"Certainly. What do you want to know?"

"What is cover?"

"Cover is the sum deposited with the broker to secure him against loss in speculative transactions, and to limit the client's liability," replied Roselle.

"Give me an instance," continued the captain.

"For instance, having reason to expect a certain stock (say Great Westerns) is likely to go up—the present price of which we will suppose is $132\frac{1}{4}$; a client sends £10 12s. 6d. as cover and commission, with instructions to buy £1,000 Great Western Railway stock."

"If it goes up?" queried Captain Dayrell, becoming much interested.

"Paying attention to the daily quotations, the operator notices that this stock rises, say to $133\frac{1}{4}\text{-}\frac{1}{2}$, and £10 or 1% is realised. If the stock rises to $134\frac{1}{4}\text{-}\frac{1}{2}$ £20 or 2% is realised, and so on in proportion."

"Should the reverse happen?"

"If, however, contrary to expectation, the stock goes down from $132\frac{1}{4}$ to $131\frac{1}{4}\text{-}\frac{1}{2}$ the "cover" has run off, and the transaction is closed with the loss of the £10 cover only. Beyond this, and the commission of 1-16th, or 12s. 6d. per £1,000 stock, there is no further liability; and the beauty of the thing is, you only lose what cover you put up."

"Suppose I put on more cover before it is too late?"

"Then you can keep the account open," replied Roselle.

"It is simple enough, and very fair," remarked Captain Dayrell.

"Yes; it limits the liability of the operator."

"I see. He can choose any stock he pleases to operate in; and, if his judgment is sound, or his information good, the profit is certain."

"Exactly," said Roselle, with a smile.

"I can see. The profits may be very large, whilst the loss is always small," remarked the captain.

"You are an apt pupil," replied Roselle, nodding approvingly

"It all depends on the operator's judgment?" continued the captain.

"And luck," answered Roselle. "But let me make it perfectly clear. You can avail yourself of the slightest variation in the market in your favour, if only $\frac{1}{8}$, whereas the market must go against you at least to the extent of the cover deposited before a loss is incurred; thus the £10 12s. 6d. commands £1,000 stock without any further charge or liability whatever."

"How can luck influence the matter?" asked Dayrell.

"I'll give you an instance of it."

"Something that occurred to you?"

"Yes," replied Roselle. "I sold Brighton A's in the teeth of a strong 'bull' market. The weather was lovely. It was the eve of the holidays. All at once came a thunderstorm. There was beastly weather for three days."

"I see."

"Traffics *nil*, and then came an accident on the line."

"That suited you."

"The price went down with a run."

"But with a £10 stake do you mean to say a fortune can be made?" pursued the captain.

"Yes."

"Give me an instance of that."

"I know a man who sold Canadian Pacifics at 66," answered Roselle, "and closed the account at 40. That is 26 per cent. profit."

"How much did he have open?"

"£5,000 stock."

"And this is the gospel according to Roselle?"

"It's the gospel according to Capel Court," replied Arthur. "But," he added, "mind this : when you operate, look out for a decent and honest broker. There are many who will take your money and never pay; and, above all, read the money article in *Truth*."

All this time Dayrell and Rosey continued to exchange glances. He thought she was worthy of a better position, and in the loyalty of his heart he pitied her. He was simple; he was generous to a fault; but he had a large and noble heart. Poor Dayrell ! That was the cause of half his troubles.

"I have an uncle a stockbroker," said Captain Dayrell, "and have heard something of this before, but never understood it."

"What is his name ?" inquired Roselle.

"Chadwick, of Threadneedle Street."

"Indeed. Isn't he enormously wealthy ?"

"I should think so ; but he's a miser. The meanest man in fact that ever lived. He hasn't spoken to me since I drove up to his house in a cab."

"Oh !"

"Fact, my dear fellow. He said I ought to have taken a 'bus to his street, and got out at the corner."

"We must utilise him," remarked Roselle, as if talking to himself.

Captain Dayrell thanked him for the trouble he had taken in imparting this information, and their conversation assumed a more confidential tone.

They seemed to have known one another for years instead of hours.

"If I had £500," said Roselle, suddenly, "I'd make £10,000."

"I can command that sum," replied Dayrell.

"Will you give up soldiering, go in with me, and ask no questions ?"

"Get my leave extended ?"

"Yes."

Captain Dayrell looked at Rosey, and thought he could do anything to be always near her.

He was falling in love.

"I'll tell you to-morrow," he replied.

"No; give me an answer now."

Arthur Roselle believed in striking while the iron was hot.

"But ——"

"Yes or no?"

For a moment more Dayrell hesitated.

He looked at Rosey again; their eyes met; he was lost.

"Yes," he answered, draining his tumbler desperately.

He had taken a leap in the dark.

Roselle got up, and grasped his hand cordially.

"It is a bargain," he exclaimed; "I shall hold you to it."

Captain Dayrell had committed himself to more than he had any idea of.

Presently Arthur went out, and Dayrell found himself sitting on the sofa by the side of Rosey, to whom he began to make love in the most marked manner.

"I am so grateful to you, for promising to assist my brother," remarked Rosey.

"I think he deserves help," replied Dayrell.

He was encouraged by her bright glances, for she was not shy or chary of bestowing them.

"Arthur requires helping. He wants some one to keep him up to the mark," she went on.

"I will be his backer."

"And you will stay with us?"

"For a time. I must get a prolongation of my leave of absence. A doctor's certificate will do that. Shall I be able to go into town to-morrow?"

"I should wait a day or two," said Rosey.

"Do you know I feel as if I could do anything for your brother. I have taken quite a liking to him," observed Dayrell.

"Everybody likes him," Rosey answered.

It was late when they separated.

On the following day he awoke with a headache, and a vivid recollection of his promise to Roselle. But in his sober senses he resolved to carry out to the utmost his undertaking for the benefit of the brother and sister.

For two days he remained in the house, being waited upon with great solicitude by Rosey, who paid him every attention.

At length he went out in a cab ; saw a doctor ; wrote to his colonel ; got his letters and some pressing bills at the club ; and sold out the £500 Government Stock, of which he had spoken, handing the proceeds to Arthur, according to their agreement.

At the club he received a letter from a favourite sister, who had not married well, informing him that her husband had lost his situation, and they were on the verge of starvation. She concluded with an appeal for assistance.

Dayrell mentioned this fact to Roselle, saying that at the first opportunity he must send something to his sister.

On his way back from town he had forwarded her a little to go on with, and tide her over her immediate necessities.

He had also bought a handsome ring for Rosey, and a beautiful bouquet of flowers. The rest of the money he scrupulously gave to his new friend.

Rosey was delighted with her presents, and the simple-minded Dayrell was as happy as a child.

He was always generous, and would give a flower girl in the street his last shilling for a penny bunch of violets.

His passion for Rosey was an infatuation.

Roselle noticed and encouraged this, and lost no time in putting his design into execution. He took a small office in the city, painting up his name, and calling himself "a financial agent." He opened an account at a well-known bank, and drew cheques, spending money without doing any business.

His partner was astonished at the delay ; but when his eye got well they visited theatres, drove to Richmond and other places to dinner, Rosey always accompanying them, and the money went like water. Although it had not been actually arranged, it was tacitly understood that Rosey and Dayrell were engaged.

At last Dayrell had his suspicions aroused, and thinking that Roselle was imposing upon him, took the bull by the horns, and spoke to him.

"Our money is going," he remarked ; "how are we to replace it ? "

Roselle showed him his pass book.

£150 had been drawn out in different cheques in a fortnight.

"Haven't you enjoyed yourself?" asked Roselle.

"Very much. I am only thinking what we shall do when it is all gone."

"You want to increase the account, to pay your bill at the club, to keep your sister?"

"Certainly. Suppose I take some money, and try my luck in operating in stocks. I haven't forgotten the lesson you gave me."

"Wait a while; you shall do that soon. At present I require your services."

"I don't understand."

"Take a *belladonna*. It's soothing," said Roselle, offering him the box.

"Don't chaff. Let us get to work. Here we are paying a clerk and running an office, and doing nothing. You are only at the office an hour or two a day, sometimes not at all."

"Very well. We will begin to-day. Go and buy a wig."

"A what?"

"An old man's wig. Did you ever play in private theatricals?"

"Often."

"Get up as an old man of reputable appearance. Borrow the clothes at a costumier's, and return them when you have done your business."

"What am I to do?" inquired Dayrell, in perplexity.

"Present this cheque at the bank."

Roselle gave him one for £375, signed by himself.

"Isn't that rather an awkward signature of yours?" asked Dayrell.

"Yes, rather."

"Will they pay on it?"

"I hope so."

"Suppose they won't?"

"Then you must come in a cab to me with the cashier. I'll be at the office to verify it."

"Suppose, again, they do pay on it?" continued Dayrell.

"All well and good."

"But what do we want with so much money?"

"To open an account at another bank."

"Really, I am in the dark."

"My dear fellow, if they won't pay, I'll put it all right for you," exclaimed Roselle, "and if they do they will be sorry for it."

"Why?"

"Because the reputable old gentleman will have presented a forgery. I shall swear it is not my signature. Compare it with others of mine, and they will have to replace the money to my account."

"Good God!" gasped Dayrell.

He looked aghast at his partner, who regarded him with a confident smile.

"That is—a—excuse me, swindling," he said.

"Precisely."

"I don't like it."

"Then we must part. You will never see Rosey again, nor will you pay your bills, or save your sister from starvation," answered Roselle, coolly.

These threats frightened Dayrell. The unfortunate young man was so much under the spell of her bewitching eyes that he could not bear the idea of giving her up, and he loved his sister.

But he remembered that he was a gentleman, and he remained firm.

"Never," he exclaimed. "We will part."

He got up and took his hat. This was not what Roselle wanted.

"Hold on," he cried. "Where are you off to? I was only chaffing."

"It was an odd kind of a joke," replied Dayrell, wiping the perspiration from his brow. "Don't do it again."

Roselle laughed the matter off, but he did not give up the plan. Finding Dayrell would not be his tool, he got Daddy to work for him. This pliant old ruffian readily consented to do as Roselle instructed him, and the plot was put into execution. In a couple of hours' time an elderly gentleman presented the cheque at the bank. It was paid. When the pass book was made up, Roselle represented that the cheque was a forgery, and the bank again placed the money to his account. All efforts to discover the old gentleman were in vain.

The trick was repeated again and again at nearly every leading bank in Europe, Daddy assuming all sorts of disguises, until the confederates had got together £10,000.

They deemed it prudent to stop there.

Arthur Roselle's brain, however, was still at work.

He represented to his dupe that he had made large sums of money by speculating on their joint account, and bought £5,000 worth of Brazilian Bonds, which he instructed Captain Dayrell to deposit for safe keeping with his rich uncle, the stockbroker of Threadneedle Street, as he was going abroad.

This was true. Roselle, Dayrell and Rosey went to Paris. Dayrell's love suit was progressing favourably. He and Rosey were engaged, though no day had been fixed for the marriage. They had only indulged in one quarrel, and that was when he met her one evening walking in the park with Tom Nash, the billiard marker. She excused herself by saying that he was an old friend of her brother's, and the affair passed off, being forgotten.

"As if she could care for such a cad as that," he comforted himself by saying.

In Paris Roselle made Captain Dayrell write to his uncle for the bonds, telling him to say that he was going on to Constantinople. They were duly forwarded by post. During the ensuing fortnight, Roselle occupied himself in forging copies of them. When this was done, he caused Dayrell, who knew nothing of the trick, to send the forgeries back to his uncle to be a second time taken care of, as he had changed his mind about going further.

A month was now spent in Paris.

Then Roselle sold the genuine bonds, and they returned to London. The next day he despatched Dayrell into the city to borrow £4,000 on the forgeries from his uncle, which he succeeded in doing.

Roselle had now about £13,000 at his command.

Captain Dayrell pressed for a share of the money, and his speedy union with Rosey, expressing his determination to go to Australia, and there settle in business of some kind. The conversation about this took place at breakfast, at the West End hotel where they were stopping. Roselle replied that he would go into the city, get the money, and divide it. Dayrell and Rosey went for a drive. On their return they found a letter from Roselle, which greatly disconcerted both of them. It contained a cheque for £100, and stated that the writer had started for the south of France, taking all the money with him. Roselle made no excuse, and offered no explanation, although he coolly informed him that he had swindled the banks, and forged the bonds which Mr. Chadwick held. He abandoned his sister to her fate as coolly as he did Dayrell.

Dayrell was furious. He saw that he had been used as a mere tool. Roselle had taken advantage of his childish simplicity, and he was left to fight the battle, after having ruined him. Some day his uncle would find out the forgeries; then would come Nemesis! Still Rosey was left him; that was one consolation. The world was not all hollow after all!

Holding the letter in his trembling hands, after they had both read it, he said—" We must begin life anew in some far-off land, my Rosey!"

"Speak for yourself," she replied, curtly.

"Are you not going to be my wife?"

"Why should I marry a man without a penny?"

"But, surely, you will not throw me up because your brother has acted the part of a scoundrel?"

"You needn't abuse my brother," she said.

"No; but——"

"Really, Captain Dayrell, I cannot listen to such rubbish," interrupted Rosey. "If you could afford to keep a wife, I would marry you as I have promised; but it is scarcely fair to ask me to wed a beggar."

He drew his breath with difficulty.

Oh! how hard it was to hear such cruel words from those lips.

"You want money," he said, slowly, like a man waking from a bad dream.

"Of course I do; every girl does."

"Or you will not marry me?"

"No. I'm not going to work for any man," she replied, tossing her head.

"Very well. I will get it for you."

"How?"

"Never mind. How long will you give me?"

"A week."

"Shall you stay here?"

"No. I shall go to my aunt's."

"Where is that?" he asked.

"In Chelsea. She keeps a lodging-house. Here is the address."

She hastily wrote down the name and address: Royal Avenue, Chelsea. He knew where it was, and put it away in his pocket.

"You shall see me in a week," he exclaimed, putting on his hat and gloves. "I'll pay the bill here."

"Don't do anything rash," she found it in her heart to say.

"I'm going to try my luck," Dayrell replied, with a hard laugh.

"In what way?"

"I haven't forgotten the lesson your amiable brother gave me in stock dealing."

"That —— !"

She spoke contemptuously, as if she had not much faith in his making any money on the Stock Exchange.

Without offering to kiss her, or even shake her hand, he quitted the room, and took a cab into the City, going direct to his uncle's office.

This gentleman was an old-fashioned broker, who had a horror of recording instruments. He had neither a tape or a telephone in his office, and did all his business in the "House," which was close to his place.

Captain Dayrell had no knowledge of stocks.

His uncle was rather surprised at his announcement that he was going to operate; but he knew nothing about his affairs, and thought he had money. At all events there was still a margin of £1,000 on the bonds he held, so he consented to act for him.

Dayrell bought three stocks at random. He was trusting entirely to luck. It was with him just like putting money on the red or the white at the tables.

Before he left the office that afternoon he had a balance in his favour.

Next day he was early on hand, driving up in a hansom with a big cigar in his mouth and a flower in his buttonhole. People wondered who he was. He bought and sold recklessly. Everything he touched went right. It was as if he could not make a mistake.

So it went on for a week.

At the end of that time he had made the nice little sum of £20,000, which he drew, and went on his way to Chelsea rejoicing. It was capital enough for a start in anything, and Rosey had more than once expressed a fancy for sheep farming in Australia. His heart beat high. She was his now, for he could raise her above want.

She received him coldly, he thought, in the dingy parlour; but her eyes brightened when he told her of his success, and how it was done.

"£20,000!" she exclaimed; "and all made on the Stock Exchange in a week."

"Yes, every shilling."

"Is it for me?"

"All," he replied. "Take it. Keep it. I will buy a licence, and to-morrow at half-past ten I shall come and claim my bride."

"I shall be ready."

"We will go overland to Naples, and take the steamer from there to Australia. It touches there."

"As you like."

"Kiss me."

She offered him her lips, and after he had kissed her tenderly, he gave her the cheque.

"There, dearest, are you satisfied?" he asked.

"Quite!" she answered, adding, "To-morrow I will be yours."

He took leave of her, and went away to make all the preparations for their marriage next day.

"After all, she was right," he muttered. "She would have been a fool to marry me without a penny, but now she's got £20,000, and can have nothing to grieve over."

That night he scarcely closed his eyes.

When he got up he dressed himself carefully. It had

been arranged that the pew opener and her husband should be the witnesses of the ceremony, which was to take place at St. Martin's-in-the-Fields.

All was provided for; nothing had been neglected.

At half-past ten he drove in a hired brougham to Royal Avenue, and knocked at the door, which was opened by an elderly lady.

"Are you Miss Roselle's aunt?" he asked.

"I am," was the reply.

"Is she ready?"

"Ready for what?"

"We are to be married this morning," said Captain Dayrell, with a *debonnair* look.

"Married?"

"Yes."

"I don't think so."

The captain started as if he had been shot, and his face went ghastly white.

"Eh, what?" he cried, catching hold of the railings to support himself.

"There must be some mistake," replied the woman. "Rosey was married two days ago to little Tom Nash, the billiard-marker—he that was her old sweetheart. They left here last evening to go and join her brother Arthur somewhere in France. I think you've got it mixed up, young man; or else she's been amusing herself at your expense. I did hear there was a young swell after her, and they used to laugh a lot, but —— Hallo! whatever is the matter with the man?"

Captain Dayrell had fallen down on the steps at her feet, and was tugging at his necktie, while inarticulate noises came from his foam-covered lips.

* * * * *

A year has passed.

Captain Dayrell, of H.M. 190th Regiment of the Line, is walking along the Marine Parade, at Brighton, with a pretty little woman hanging on his arm, and looking up lovingly in his face through the bright sunshine. The band is playing; the sea breaking in surf on the beach, and a clear blue sky is overhead.

It is his wife, for he has married the colonel's daughter, who had long loved him.

"What a fool I was," he thinks, as he returns the little woman's loving look. "Fancy a fellow wanting to throw himself away on a girl like Rosey. How could I have been such a fool with such a woman."

He had paid his debts and redeemed the forged bonds, without discovery. His uncle had died leaving him a legacy of £10,000, with which he honourably indemnified the banks that had been defrauded by Roselle's trickery; and, by judicious speculation, he was in a fair way of amassing a tolerable fortune on the Stock Exchange.

* * * * * *

Another year has passed.

Two men are on trial at the Old Bailey. One is proved to have defrauded the Bank of England of a large sum; the other has stabbed his wife mortally, in a fit of jealousy, aggravated by drunken frenzy.

They are Arthur Roselle, and Tom Nash, the billiard marker, who married Rosey.

The slender thread is cut; the heavy sword has fallen.

THE MISSING BROKER,

OR

THE SCHEMER'S FATE.

THE MISSING BROKER,

OR

THE SCHEMER'S FATE.

CAPTAIN RAMSDEN, half-pay, retired, a *bon vivant*, and good fellow generally, was entertaining his friends at luncheon at the City Carlton. He speculated, as most men do nowadays when they have a little spare cash to play with. As he always looked on the bright side of things, he was naturally a "bull." His liver was in good order, he never took anybody's pills, and found plenty of exercise as good as medicine. The markets were good. When he left Wardrobe Chambers the English Funds were very strong, and other stocks, as usual, took their tone from Consols. English railways were in good demand. Chatham Preference were up. There had been no accident on the line lately. No one thought of alluding to it as the London Smashem and Turn-the-lot-over Railway. Metropolitan and the two Southern lines were in request. No one had started a scarlatina scare at Ramsgate; no family had been poisoned by eating mackerel at Margate; and it was satisfactory to learn that the drainage of Brighton was all that could be desired. Great Northern A showed a considerable advance. From the other side, Readings, Louisville, Pacifics, Eries and Trunks were better. Vanderbilt and Jay Gould had shaken hands over a bottle of Pommery Sec.

Jim Keene had said "There should be no more cutting of rates," and James Gordon Bennett had left Atlantic Cables alone for a time. The "bull" was lying down with the "bear," and there had been a general shaking of hands all round at Delmonico's and the Brunswick. Sheridan Shook had stood drinks in honour of Cleveland at the Windsor, and nobody fired a shot at either Pacific Mail or Western Union. Mexican Rails had risen two per cent. Only one President had been killed lately in that highly volcanic but dangerously romantic republic, and the Mexicanos had not indulged in more than three revolutions and two pronunciamentos in the last six months. Maximilian's bones rested in peace at Queretaro, and the fate of the invader was not flaunted in the faces of the foreigner more than seven times a week by the daily newspapers. And as the gallant captain had many irons in the fire, he had invited three friends to form a *parti carré* ; the viands were excellent, the wines beyond reproach, especially Watchter's '74, which was unexceptionable, but the weather for May was abominable. At two o'clock it had clouded over, and rain was falling persistently. Cigars and Burgundy were the order of the day, and it was unanimously decided that business should be considered over.

"I for one shall not go back to the office," said Ramsden; "and if you fellows like, I'll tell you a story about a dishonest broker. It is a tale of long ago, but I daresay you have heard of Gilman French."

"Yes," replied Mr. Gaylor, a merchant well known on 'Change, who was one of the guests. "He was a defaulter, and shot himself on Hampstead Heath."

"He did not."

"But they found the body."

"I don't care for that. He's alive now, and that's part of the story," said the captain. "I knew him well, for I was a customer of his."

"Ah! you can go back a long way," remarked Gaylor.

"I should think I could," replied Captain Ramsden, with a knowing shake of the head.

Mr. Gaylor was a fidgety man.

It was very difficult to keep him still ; he objected to

being anchored, as he called it, and though he wanted to hear the story, he could not help looking at his watch.

"Put that timekeeper of yours up," said the captain.

"Time flies," replied Gaylor. "Ah! I often think that my business would go to the devil if I were dead."

"Should you take it with you?" asked Ramsden, slyly.

At this sally there was a roar of laughter.

"That's too bad," replied Gaylor; "'pon my word, that's going a little too far."

"So you'll say, before you get to the end of your journey."

"Come now."

His remark was cut short by another burst of merriment.

"It's getting hot," said Mr. Rothery, one of the guests.

"Well," answered Ramsden, who was incorrigible, "the climate of the place he's talking about is generally regarded as sultry."

"It is not business altogether that calls me," explained Gaylor, when the laughter excited at his expense had somewhat subsided.

"What then?"

"I had promised Bevan, the lawyer, to go with him to see the new picture. By Jove! Ramsden, you ought to take that in."

"What is it?"

"The Triumph of the Innocents."

"Not I."

"Why?"

"The Triumph of the Three per Cents. would be more in my line."

"What for?" inquired Gaylor.

"Because I'm a 'bull' of Consols, my boy," replied the captain, amid another burst of laughter.

After a pause, Gaylor sat down.

"That's right," continued Ramsden, "make your miserable life happy by listening to my story."

"I hope I shall survive the infliction," answered Gaylor, who wanted to say something by way of revenge.

"It will make you grow fat, and you will look less as if you were walking about to save funeral expenses."

"Stop chaffing, and go on then."

"I was about when Sir John Dean Paul," began Ramsden, "made a mess of the Royal British Bank. I can remember Roupell—the forger—dined with him lots of times when he was member for Lambeth, and Redpath, of the Great Northern, who robbed the company and bought pictures and statuary by the old masters, with his ill-gotten gains. Very much more recently, I call to mind Black Friday, when Overend and Gurneys smashed up, the largest discount house the world ever saw, gentlemen; and when there was the run on the Agra and Masterman's, the City went mad. Wall Street, in New York, could not have shown anything like it with gold at 190, and rising at that, with no help from the Secretary of the Treasury at Washington. Yes, gentlemen, I've seen as much as most men; but to the story, the tale's the thing, eh?"

There was not a dissentient voice; every man filled his glass, and lit a fresh cigar.

"Carried *nem. con.*, as Gladstone said of his Franchise Bill. I must begin by telling you that this man, Gilman French, had a splendid business, and stood A 1. His paper was gilt edged, his clients were as numerous as the sand on the sea-shore—pardon a little hyperbole—and the list of the securities in which he dealt as long as Homer's catalogue of ships. But he had two families; that is where the mischief began. His wife lived in a small house at Kensington, and wore a stuff dress. She studied economy, being a plain, simple, honest-hearted, good woman, whom French ought to have prized for her many virtues more than he did. She did not appear in a blaze of diamonds. She was not weighed down with jewellery, her wedding-ring was enough for her. A drive in the park in a modest brougham was all she allowed herself, and a cook and a housemaid supplied her domestic wants. The other one, with whom I had the pleasure of being acquainted, resided in a villa at Fulham, and if possible she outdid all the other *Messalinas* of the West-End in display, dress, and extravagance generally. Her horses, her jewels, her wines were superb, and she spent money with a lavish hand. They all do—those butterflies. She was originally a dancer at the Hyde Park Theatre, known in the bills as La Favorita; that was where Gilman French first met her. It was a bad day's work for him. I have generally found that a business man may date the commencement of his decline and fall to the contraction of an illicit connection of this kind, and though Estelle (she was of Spanish extraction, and that was her name) was very fascinating, she undoubtedly ruined Gilman French, who was one of the smartest men on the London Stock Exchange. Seldom has a man of intelligence and mature age been so infatuated with a woman as French was with La Favorita. Of an imperious disposition, she took advantage of his weakness, and ordered him about like a dog. All women love power; they are by nature tyrants; and she was a Nero or a Caligula in petticoats. Her tempests of passion were terrible. One day he was to dine with her, and had promised her a valuable picture. It was one by the French artist Solomon. He gave £600 for it, at Leggat's. Somehow he was an hour late."

"I suppose the dinner was spoiled?" said Gaylor.

"Yes, and so was the picture."

"How?"

"She took up a knife," replied Ramsden, "and ripped it all to pieces. But to resume. Her demands upon his purse were incessant. On the Black Friday I have mentioned, he was hit hard by the Gurneys', but there was no cessation in the extravagance of La Favorita. I fancy it was about that time that he began to go wrong. That she deceived him, was a matter of course. He could not be always with her, and there was a certain Count de Villa Franca, who was seen with her in the park and at the opera. Amongst her extravagances, just to give you an idea of the woman's disposition, I may mention something she did for a dog. It was a poodle. All her affection seemed to be centred on this wretched little animal, who was called Folette—in fact, we christened her *la Maison Folette.* But what do you think? She actually had a kennel made for it of pure, solid gold, worth ever so much. I believe, at her sale, it was bought by the Duchess of W It was said that she slept in black satin sheets. It began to be whispered about that French was operating on his own account, as well as acting and opening stock for clients, and the jobbers began to look upon him with suspicion and made him wide prices, or else they turned their backs upon him. There was no diminution in the expenditure, and Favorita's balls and parties was still the talk of the town. An old gentleman, by name Evans, had his suspicions aroused. He had entrusted our broker with securities valued at £100,000, and one fine morning he called for them. French had hypothecated them to the Metropolitan and District Bank, for advances made to him from time to time, and was unable to produce them. He asked for time.

"'You are an old friend,' said Evans, 'I have known you honourably for a long time, and have trusted you with my property, partly as cover for my transactions, and partly for the sake of security, though the property would have been as safe at my banker's as with you. Now, I want to strike a balance and close the account ; there is no friendship in business. I will give you until to-morrow.'

"'Your bonds and shares are all right,' replied French.

"'That may be. I am making no objection ; all I say is, let me have my property'

"'Very well ; call to-morrow,' said the broker, with a forced smile ; 'everything shall be ready for you.'

"Gilman French for the next hour tried every means in his power to get the money to release those securities, but without success. He saw that the game was up. Evans, by putting on the screw, had compassed his ruin. A criminal charge stared him in the face. He saw no way out of the difficulty, and was driven to his wits' end. It was three o'clock in the afternoon on a beautiful June day. He had been in the House, and it was afterwards remarked by the jobbers that his manner and appearance had undergone a great change since the morning. Now occurred a most extraordinary thing.

"A gentleman who gave the common name of Smith asked to see him, and was admitted to his private room. This man had just arrived from New Zealand, where he had been a sheep farmer. He had no relations, and knew nobody in this country. With him he had £50,000. Some one had recommended him to apply to Gilman French, who would invest it for him to the best advantage. He had driven from the docks to his office. French looked upon this as a veritable godsend. He took the money, giving a receipt for it, and asked the party of the name of Smith to come and see him the next day."

"Pardon me," interrupted Mr. Gaylor. "I should like to ask you a question."

"Certainly," responded Captain Ramsden.

"Do the public usually put securities like that with a broker?"

"Yes."

"Isn't it foolish to do so?"

"Not at all foolish, if he doesn't re-hypothecate them."

"How can they tell?"

"By asking to see them at any moment," said the Captain. "But now comes the most singular part of my story.

"He then for the first time took a good look at his visitor, and was astonished to see that he bore a strong resemblance to him. They were the same age and height, and might have been taken for twin brothers. At his request the stranger stood by his side at a looking glass; the likeness was marvellous.

"'Strange thing we should be so much like each other,' he remarked. 'But it has often been said that every one has his double. The Germans call it a *doppleganger*.'

"Mr. Smith acquiesced in this; it was odd. While French was recommending an hotel to him, the stranger put his hand to his side, staggered, and breathed heavily.

"'Anything the matter?' asked French.

"'My heart,' was the reply.

"'You are not feeling unwell, I hope!'

"'I'm better now Some day I shall go off like that.'

"'Allow me to send my manager with you to—say the Manchester. Capital hotel, not far from here.'

"'Willingly,' said the stranger.

"This offer was accepted. French called Layton, his manager, and gave the old colonist into his charge. They departed together, and our friend Gilman began to think what he could do with the windfall which had so providentially come in his way It was not enough to square Evans with, and the terrible idea occurred to him of running away with it. For some time he remained plunged in thought. He was roused by the return of Layton, who looked considerably fluttered.

"'Have you seen the old gent. comfortably fixed?' he asked.

"'He's as comfortable as he ever will be,' answered Layton, significantly.

"'What do you mean?'

"'He's dead, sir!'

"'God bless me! Dead! How?—when?—where?'

"Layton proceeded to explain that when he and Mr. Smith got into a cab to go to the hotel, which was only at the top of Aldersgate Street, the latter was taken very seriously ill, and not knowing where to go, he ordered the driver to drive direct to Bartholomew's Hospital. On the way Mr. Smith became worse. He administered a stimulant, but the old man sank and died. The body was still in the cab. No address was found on him, and Layton had come back posthaste for instructions as to what should be done with the dead man.

"It happened that Layton was well acquainted with the cabman, who always stood on the same rank in Moorgate Street. For years, both French and his manager had been in the habit of employing this man, whose name was Tapp. He had invariably been well paid, and would do anything for them. Every year he had driven them down to the Derby, and they looked upon him in the light of an old servant, if not a kind of poor friend.

"'Tapp,' said Layton, as they stopped before the office, 'don't say a word to any one till I come back.'

"'Right, sir!' replied the cabman.

"'If any one asks a question, reply that the old man is asleep.'

"'Ay, ay!'

"'Imply that he has had a drop too much.'

Tapp winked his eye.

"'I understand, sir,' he replied.

"'I'll explain my——'

"'A nod is as good as a wink to a blind horse, sir,' said the cabman, cutting him short.

"It was then that an inspiration came over Gilman French. Layton had been his manager ever since he had been in business, and knew as well as his employer how affairs stood. In fact he was in his confidence, and it was no secret to him that French was in trouble. They talked long and earnestly together, and this was the result of their confabulations. The broker was to go in every direction, getting all the money he could. After dark French—disguised—was to leave for the Continent, where Layton was to join him a few days afterwards—at Brussels, I think—the master taking all the cash they could get with him. That night Layton was to perform his share in the most extraordinary plot that the most fertile brain ever hatched, and he did it.

"Layton returned to the cab, and instructed Tapp to drive to his house in the North of London, where he had a disused stable at the rear of the premises. Here the cab with the body in it was placed until nightfall. In death Mr. Smith's features looked more than ever like those of Gilman French. The few hours of daylight that remained were passed by Tapp and Layton together in making a bargain. The cabman for his services was to be paid a handsome sum, and he agreed to participate in the plot. When night came they took the cab out of the stable with the body still in it, and drove to Hampstead Heath. Here it was dressed in some old clothes of French's; cards and documents for identification were put in the pockets, and Layton, firing a pistol at the head, put a bullet in the brain. He laid the pistol by the side of the corpse, and the imposture was complete.

"The next day the body was found, and London was startled by the report of the suicide of Mr. Gilman French, the well-known stockbroker. Layton appeared at the inquest. Verdict, Suicide while in an unsound state of mind. The offices were shut up. La Favorita had a sale, and vanished to Paris, where she was last seen with Villa Franca. Mrs. French and her children were taken care of by sympathising friends, who started her daughter and herself in a ladies' school. Layton joined his confederate, the dishonest broker, and they went to Andalusia, where they are at present engaged in the wine trade."

Captain Ramsden paused to get his breath.

"And you expect us to believe that yarn?" asked one of his guests.

"Certainly. The last time I was cruising in the Mediterranean I stopped at Malaga. Here I made the acquaintance of a beautiful woman, who invited me to spend an evening at her house with her husband and herself. To my astonishment the husband was no other than Gilman French. I recognised the old boy in a moment, and had as fine a bottle of Amontillado with him as any one would wish to drink."

"What did he say?"

"Told me the whole story, and laughed at it as a good joke."

The guests looked at one another. The captain ordered some more wine, and the conversation flagged.

"Strange things happen in this city," observed Mr. Gaylor.

"Bah! that's nothing to what I could tell you," replied Ramsden. "Some day when we have time you shall thrill over my experiences."

Mr. Gaylor looked at the window, and observed that it had left off raining. Every one rose. It seemed as if they had had enough of the gallant captain's experiences for that day, and Gaylor was heard to murmur that he would take a look at his library edition of Munchausen's travels when he got home that night.

The captain was left to settle the bill. A cloud came over his face, as the waiter, an aged specimen of his race, counted the change out of a ten pound note, and he said, as if to himself, "The young men think they know everything. Now, I'll bet a fiver that those fellows did not believe a word of what I told them."

"Beg pardon, sir," said the waiter. "It's very 'ard, but I believe it."

"You?"

"Excuse me, sir, but I was waiting at your table, and 'eard the story. Waiter's privilege, you know, sir: and I knew the gentleman well, sir. Used to dine at the Baltic often and often, sir, when I was a waiter there."

"You knew Gilman French?"

"Oh, dear me, yes, sir." Knew him well. Free, open-handed gent, he was, sir. Never gave me less than 'arf-a-crown, sir, never. Thank you, sir. Good day. Much obliged, I'm sure."

Captain Ramsden had thrown two and sixpence down on the bill.

Sympathy is refreshing sometimes, even if we have to pay for it.

THE SPECULATING M.Ps.

THE SPECULATING M.Ps.

WE are not about to attack single-member constituencies, though the borough of Turnover, in Somerset, was responsible for Mr. Tite Roper, M.P., and the little town of Knockmadoon, County Kerry, Ireland, stood sponsor for Mr. Dennis Blatherem Macdermot O'Kite, M.P., who was chiefly known in Ireland as the proprietor of an incendiary sheet called the *Knockmadoon Patriot Flag*, which was published weekly. Messrs. Tite Roper and O'Kite were middle-aged bachelors, living in chambers together in King Street, Westminster, so as to be close to the House of Commons. Mr. Roper had often turned his political coat, being everything from a Conservative to a Radical, and was now a Moderate Liberal, in deference to the democratic wave which he said was flowing over the country. O'Kite was a Home Ruler, though he did not always vote with his party. He had his own axe to sharpen, and found it to his interest to be called Independent. Their incomes being small, they supplemented them by speculating on the Stock Exchange, by promoting companies and sitting on the boards of direction, being what are called Guinea-pigs, on several undertakings. The *Patriot Flag* brought in little but notoriety to Mr. Dennis Blatherem Macdermot O'Kite. The articles were written in London by a pensioner and hanger-on of Mr. Roper, whom he playfully called his financial Frankenstein. His name was Vernon Estcourt. He was a poor old broken-down man now, but there had been a time when Mr. Estcourt owned broad acres and was a master of foxhounds. In an evil hour he had met Tite Roper, who induced him to put his money in worthless undertakings. Roper reaped the benefit, but Estcourt went to the wall. His creditors sold everything he had, and he was glad at last to do secretarial work for the man who to his ruin had been his friend, philosopher, and guide. To add to his trouble he had imbibed a taste for drink, which at times rendered him a nuisance to the speculating M.P s, but Mr. Roper could not shake him off. Estcourt was behind the scenes, and knew too much about him; besides, he had made him what he was. If he was cursed with his financial Frankenstein it was only retributive justice, and perhaps proper that it should be so. The Macdermot O'Kite liked Estcourt because he wrote slashing articles for the *Patriot Flag*, and never begrudged him whisky, for the more he took the more his thrilling leaders were calculated to stir men s minds. The Session was just about to commence. Roper and O'Kite were in town. They had two undertakings in hand which occupied all their attention : one was the new club in St. James's, known as the Rose, Shamrock, and Thistle, of which Roper was manager and secretary. It was called for short the Rose Club. Mr. Roper's management of it during the half-year it had been in existence was seriously called in question by a party of members led by Sir Lucius Holyoake, Bart., who wanted to get rid of him, and only required special information to make grave allegations against the member for Turnover. This was alluded to in club circles as the War of the Roses. Up to the present time Roper had been too clever for his enemy, Sir Lucius, and the rest of the malcontents, though there were weak points in his armour, and he knew it. The O'Kite was responsible for the other enterprise—he owned a bog in Kerry. It was his favourite custom to speak of it as "me property, bedad." He had promoted a private bill in Parliament to enable him to form a company for the improvement of his property. It was to be named "The Great Blatherem Land Reclamation Company," and if he got his bill through the House, he and Roper were prepared to invite gentlemen of means to construct a syndicate. Affairs were in this condition a few days before the assembling of Parliament. It was a rainy, foggy, muggy afternoon, and the members sat in their joint sitting room before a blazing fire, drinking a bottle of wine and discussing their projects.

"I see the Blatherem Land's to be opposed," remarked Roper.

"By this and by that, if the Government won't support me they'll not have me vote," replied O'Kite, "and votes won't be as plintiful as blackberries wid thim this Session, I'm afther thinking."

"We shall pull it through, I think. I spoke to the Irish Secretary about it, and he promised that he would do what he could."

"Ah, bedad! the spalpeens will promise anything on the eve of a division, as they're thinking of the vote of censure the Opposition is thritening."

"I told him your constituents very much desired it."

"Me constituents," repeated The Macdermot O'Kite, with a laugh; "we've got about two hundred voters all tould, at Knockmadoon, and the principal thing they want is breeches and bread."

"Are they so poor as that?"

"Poor! they're hungry poor. The land is so bad that in places a nettle refuses to grow on it, and if Knockmadoon wasn't by the say, and the people had a bit of say fishing, be jabers, it's starving they'd be all the time instead of half; ye don't know the County Kerry, I tell ye."

"I've heard of it," replied Roper.

"Why don't ye read the *Flag* regularly? It's all set forth ivery week. I kape that poor divil av yours, Estcourt, hard at the poverty of the land, and the misery English rule has brought wid it."

"But if the land is to blame, you'd be no better off if you had Home Rule to-morrow."

"Av coorse we shouldn't. What thin?"

"Why do you keep on flogging a dead horse?"

"To throw dust in the eyes of the ilictors, me bhoy," answered O'Kite, with a knowing wink. "You wouldn't have thim belave the Britisher was their best friend; we'd git the dhirty kick out that same day, so we would."

"Ha! ha!" laughed Roper, "you know your book."

"None betther. I talk of me constituents! What are

they? The principal av thim is pigs, and the balance av thim is goats. The men and the women have gone to Ameriky. Wait till I tell yees what I did onest, and it's as thrue as I'm sitting here right forninst yees. Some ganius tould me I'd add to me income—bad cess to it for being so small as to amount to nixt to nothin' at all, at all—by kaping bays."

"What?"

"Bays; did ye niver hear of bay kapin'?"

"Not that I'm aware of," replied Mr. Tite Roper, who was sometimes puzzled by his friend's brogue and pronunciation.

"Faith! they're the crathers that make the honey. Holy Virgin, pity his Saxon ignorance this day."

"Oh, you mean bees—bee-culture. I see."

"By the piper that played before Moses, you'd aggravate a saint!" cried The Macdermot O'Kite. "Isn't it bays I've been maning all the while? Well, to cut a long story short, I sint to Corrk for some hives of them, and if they didn't all die of starvation in a month I wish I may niver taste a dhrop av whisky again. There was no flowers or clover grass for thim to live on, d'ye see, and they perished miserably, as did me poor fellow-countrymen in the famine, whin there was the disase among the praties. Oh, you've got a lot to answer for, you English."

"You're not making a speech in the House now, allow me to remind you."

"Spache, is it? Wait till ye hear me. I'll have a notice in the paper about a gravance one of me Knockmadoon supporters has against the Government. There was an excise officer standing by a fisherman an' the wind blew the fisherman's hat into the say, and it was carried out in the Atlantic bekase the exciseman wouldn't go after it."

"But it wasn't his business."

"Wasn't he a Government official? Answer me that."

"No doubt."

"An' isn't it the business of the officials to do all they can for the people? I tell yees it's a gravance, and I'll put it on the paper, as sure as my name's Dennis," answered the O'Kite, vehemently, "and I'll get that spalpeen of your's, Estcourt, to write me something for the *Flag*, which will astonish the Castle."

"You fellows are always abusing the Lord Lieutenant and the Castle," observed Roper.

"It's a nest of corruption, so it is; a whitened sepulchre, a *vile corpus*, a festering sore, a———"

"Spare me," said Roper.

"Ah, my bhoy, you don't know it so well as I do. If you want to make Oireland contented you must abolish Castledom and Flunkydom, and give us a National Parliament on College Green."

"You may have it as far as I am concerned. The business of the House would go on better without your Milesian contingent."

"You hate us; I know it. We haven't a friend on this side St. George's Channel; you're all aloike. It was only last session, when I was addressing the House and was warning the Prime Minister that the sword of Damocles was hanging over his hoary head, that a noble lord, who is rather deaf, said in me hearin', moind you, in me hearin', that he quite approved of damning O'cles, though he didn't know what borough he sat for; in fact, if he had his way he would damn all the Irish members; and when I asked the Speaker if it wasn't a breach of privilege and unparliamentary language for a mimber of that House to use, he ruled that I was out of order."

Mr. Tite Roper laughed inordinately at this story.

"We should lose all our fun without you Irishmen," he replied.

"An uncertain footstep was heard in the passage, and a voice was heard singing in a rich Irish brogue a snatch of a song.

"Hark at him," said the O'Kite, "It's that murtherin' villain Estcourt; he's drunk bedad, and he's mocking me."

"Surely he would not have the presumption."

"I tell you he is, and it makes me blood boil. Hark now! By this and by that I'll not stand it."

"'Oh! whisky you're the devil, you're leading me asthray, you're stronger far than wather and mightier than tay,'" sang the intruder, who fumbled awhile at the door before he found the handle and let himself in.

It was Estcourt; he was intoxicated, and he was mocking

Mr. Blatherem Macdermot O'Kite. In him you saw a wreck, but yet the wreck of a gentleman of education and standing who had seen better days; he was careless in his dress, he wore a shockingly bad hat, his nose was unpardonably red, and he exhaled an odour of rum and stale tobacco which was the reverse of agreeable. In this literary and secretarial hack no one would have recognised the former country landowner and M. F. H. Helping himself to a cigar, he sat down without being asked, placing himself quite on a level with the two M.P.'s.

"Have you kept yourself sober enough to prepare a balance sheet for the auditors at the next meeting of the Rose Club?" asked Mr. Roper.

In reply to this question Estcourt placed a paper on the table.

"I've cooked the accounts as you told me," answered he, "though, perhaps, the term is not an agreeable one to your ears."

"If you have come here to quarrel, my dear fellow, I shall go out and leave you, although it is my own room," said Roper.

"I've no desire to quarrel with any one. I've done my work. If I drink, it is to drown care. Here's your leader, Mr. O'Kite, telling the Lord Lieutenant he ought to put you in the commission of the peace. If I were he, I'd put you in Kilmainham, and keep you there."

"There's an insult!" cried O'Kite, angrily.

Estcourt was evidently in a combative mood, and did not care what he said; it was nothing to him whether he offended or pleased; he was simply in a temper which made him wish to annoy.

"Take it as such, if you like," he retorted.

"Bedad, it's more than me flesh and blood can bear."

"Your blood," said Estcourt, with a sneer.

"And phat'll yees be afther saying about me blood? Weren't me ancestors Kings of Oireland, before such mushrooms as yourselves were heard of? before, indade, your counthry was discovered by the Romans? I'll not take the insult from an omadhoun wid but one shirt to his back, and that not a clane one."

Fixing his lack-lustre grey eye upon him, Estcourt rose from his chair, but tottered and sank back again.

"Confound the drink, it goes to my legs," he said. "But you wouldn't talk to me like that if I was sober; however, life's too short for snarling; there's my hand, if you like to take it. If you don't, you can leave it alone."

The Irishman was warm-hearted, as all his race are, and wasn't to be outdone in generosity. Estcourt chaffed him at times unmercifully, and he resented it. Neither he nor Roper wanted to make an enemy of the man, because he knew too much about them, and could have ventilated unpleasant facts to their prejudice. He had been sent over to Ireland to report on the Knockmadoon Land, and knew it was only a worthless bog that could never be reclaimed. He knew that Roper had, as manager of the Rose Club, paid himself a larger salary than the committee had ever authorised, and he had, indeed, helped himself to money which Sir Lucius Holyoake could make him disgorge, if he could not prosecute him criminally, should the actual state of affairs ever come to his knowledge.

"Arrah, be aisy now," exclaimed O'Kite. "At times ye've no more manners than a Connaught pig, saving your prisence, but you don't mane it. There's me hond. Shake, man, shake! and it's meself that's to blame for not asking if ye've got a mouth on yees, as we say in Knockmadoon, whin the bhoys mate wid one another at the sbebeen."

They shook hands, patching up a peace, and Estcourt did not require much persuasion to sodden himself still more with whisky and water.

"Where have you been all day, Vernon?" inquired Mr. Roper.

"I was at work all the morning," replied the hack. "I can't sleep after I wake. Perhaps you think I spent the rest of the day in a public-house, but I didn't. I met an old friend, who is now a high Indian official. He's home on leave."

"Did he give yees the could shoulder?" asked O'Kite.

"No, Dennis O'Blatherem, he did not. He's a gentleman, and he felt sorry for me. He gave me a dinner at the Empire Club, if you want to know, and we talked politics.

He's seen the draft of the Queen's speech. There's likely to be trouble with Russia, if she pushes any further into Afghanistan. Troops are to be concentrated at Jellalabad and Quetta. Ministers are going to show a firm front for once."

"Is that true?"

"Do you think I'd tell you so, if it wasn't?"

"I mean," said Roper, "is the information reliable?"

"Yes," replied Estcourt. "The reserves are to be called out and the militia embodied."

"By Jove! I'll act upon that," said Roper. "I'll sell a 'put' of Consols. There is nothing like doing an option in Consols when the political horizon is obscured."

"And I'll sell Russians, bedad, as sure as Saint Patrick of blessed memory drove snakes out of Ireland," remarked O'Kite.

"I don't understand the Stock markets," observed Estcourt, "but I'll tell you what is going to win the Lincoln Handicap, the Liverpool Grand National, and the University Boat Race."

"That's too risky for me. I like to act on information," replied Roper.

"And I back public form."

"Did you ever win anything?"

"I have won and I have lost, though I am one of those unlucky beggars that generally gets hold of the wrong end of the stick."

"Ah, that's not like me," said O'Kite. "It's a cold day when I'm left, and if I touch anything it's sure to turn to gold. There is the Knockmadoon property. If we can only get the capital to reclaim the land I'll be rich."

"You will, but how about the shareholders?"

"It's illegant soil, I'm telling yees. It'll grow corrn and praties equally well. I have no hesitation in saying that when it is properly drained there will not be a finer estate anywhere."

"You forget I've seen it, and it's nothing but bog," said Estcourt; "you can't drain it; the thing is a swindle from beginning to end."

Mr. Tite Roper looked annoyed.

"That is a word we never allow to be uttered here," he exclaimed, pompously; "you are very irritating to-day, Estcourt, and you will oblige me very much by going home."

"I'm not going," was the obstinate answer.

"How would you like to be called names?"

"I never swindled anybody. I've been the victim, and you both know it. At one time I could buy and sell you a dozen times over. If the cap fits wear it, that's all I've got to say."

"Afther that, if you don't go I'll be the one to make yees," cried O'Kite.

"Don't be rash," said Roper.

"I think I'm right in saying that these rooms are as much mine as yours, sorr, and I'll not endure any more balderdash from this fellow. Out wid yees! Double quick march! Holy shmoke! I can't bear it; and I couldn't, and I wouldn't, be jabers, if all the lawyers in the Four Courts were to rise up against me."

He seized Estcourt by the nape of the neck, and dragged him to the door. He was too far gone to offer any resistance, and was finally ejected into the street. The apartments being on the ground floor, he fell violently against a lamp-post, helped along by a blow from the Irish M.P.

The assault, the blow, the cool air combined sobered him. For a moment he had a strong inclination to follow O'Kite into the house, but he resisted it. Rising, he picked up his hat, and his face became convulsed with rage.

"What!" he gasped, "kicked out by a blatherskite like that! a rank Irish adventurer, who is not fit to black my boots! A blow! My God! have I fallen so low? I, Vernon Estcourt, who used to hold his head as high as a prince! I shall go mad! It can't be true! I'm dreaming! No, no, I must not deceive myself!"

He paused, and looking at the window, shook his fist.

"Revenge!" he added; "I will live for it. Not another drop of liquor passes my lips. Sot! fool! I deserve it all; but, so help me, high Heaven, I will have my revenge!"

Putting up the collar of his coat, for the winds of early February are apt to bite shrewdly, he darted round a corner and was soon lost to sight.

When Mr. Dennis O'Blatherem Macdermot O'Kite returned to the room he found Mr. Tite Roper looking greatly displeased.

"I've put the blayguard out," he exclaimed, "and I ought to be afther washing my hands after touching such a thafe of the worrld,—bad cess to the haythen!"

"It strikes me you've done a bad day's work for both of us," replied the member for Turnover.

"An' why should yees say that?"

"I've known Estcourt longer than you have. He's got the blood and breeding of a gentleman. I'm sure he'll never forgive such treatment. It isn't in his nature to look over an assault like that."

"Be aisy," replied O'Kite. "Isn't he a man in chains?"

"What do you mean?"

"I mane that he won't think av the tratement whin he wakes up in the mornin' and wants the price av a dhrink. The potheen's a fetish wid him. He'll want his hire money. Don't we pay him and kape him?"

"Well, we shall see."

With these oracular words, Roper went to dress for dinner. The Government had sent out a strong whip to their supporters. The Secretary to the Treasury had invited both Roper and O'Kite to a dinner party that evening, and though they knew it to be a political ruse they were going, as it added to their dignity and importance.

It turned out that the member for Knockmadoon was mistaken in his estimate of Estcourt's character. The next day he did not appear in King Street, nor the day after. They sent to his lodgings after him, for they wanted him to do some work. He had left without giving his new address, and we will follow him.

The night of his degradation he spent in bed. He awoke with a splitting headache, but he eschewed his usual pick-me-up—a couple of sodas and brandy. His nerves were greatly shaken, so he took a little chloral and went for a long walk. In the afternoon he called upon his friend from India, who had told him to let him know if he wanted any assistance. On this friend's mercy he threw himself, confessing that he had lost himself through idleness and excessive indulgence, which he was determined to give up as long as he lived. The friend lent him a helping hand in the crisis of his fate. He lent him money, he took him to a tailor, and he engaged fresh lodgings for him. A week passed. Vernon Estcourt became a man. A miracle seemed to have been worked in his favour. The longing for liquor went away. He became lithe, agile, active again. Well dressed, with money in his pocket and the promise of a colonial appointment if he did not fall again within three months, he held himself erect, for he had gained his self-respect which had been so long in abeyance. Nor was his brain idle. He had not forgotten the vow he had made in his anguish on that dreadful night, when he was thrown into the street like a pariah dog and struck like a tramp.

He sought an interview with the Secretary for Ireland, and gave him all the information he possessed about the Knockmadoon estate. The O'Kite had actually had the audacity to ask for a Government subsidy to assist the company in reclaiming his bog, and so anxious were ministers to conciliate the Irish and win their votes that the request was seriously entertained until the whole facts of the impudent imposture were placed before them.

"That's one spoke in their wheel," he muttered.

He then went to the M.P.'s broker.

"You act for Mr. Roper, I believe," he said.

"I do," was the reply.

"When he operates you require cover?"

"Of course."

"How do you take it?"

"In cheques."

"Be cautious about his cheques. That is all I have to say."

When Mr. Roper called again the broker declined to act for him, unless for cash.

His next act was to pay a visit to Sir Lucius Holyoake at the Three Countries Club, otherwise the Rose, Shamrock and Thistle, which ought to have been a very prosperous concern if it had been managed properly. The following day was the one appointed for the audit and committee meeting for the examination of accounts, which had been hopelessly mixed up, entangled, and falsified by Mr. Tite Roper, who hoped to be able to pay back the balance he had abstracted during the summer, if he could put off exposure on this occasion. It was not a proprietary club, and every member was individually interested in it's not getting into debt; but it had got into debt to upholsterers, billiard table makers, wine merchants, cigar dealers and others. Mr. Roper had had the money and played ducks and drakes with it, yet, as we have stated, he hoped to put the affairs of the club straight, if something turned up during the summer, and he had so many irons in the fire that he thought he could surely rely upon some of them being trumps. He made a little money by his option, but not much, as Russia drew in her horns at the determined attitude of England, and the scare was over for a time. Sir Lucius Holyoake and a few friends had an inkling of how the club was being mismanaged, but as Roper held a position and knew such a number of the members, Sir Lucius and his followers were in a hopeless minority if it came to a vote even in committee. What he wanted was a plain statement of facts and figures, and this was just what Vernon Estcourt was ready to give him. On his way to the club he met Roper and O'Kite walking arm-in-arm. They looked rather the worse for wear, having been in the House till two o'clock in the morning, after which they played unlimited loo in Arlington Street till the milk came to the door. It was, as Roper said, burning the candle at both ends and in the middle. Estcourt was as fresh as paint and resembled a highly trained three-year old, ready and fit to run for a man's life. Staring at them with a well bred insolence he knew how to assume—none better—he passed by without taking any notice.

"Estcourt," said Roper.

There was no answer.

"My dear fellow, stop a minute," continued the member for Turnover, running after him, with O'Kite by his side.

"I don't know you, sir," replied Estcourt, drawing himself up proudly.

"I'm Roper, and this is O'Kite, members for Turnover and Knockmadoon, you know; you used to work for us. There is a balance due to you. Come somewhere and have a glass of wine, and I will give you a cheque."

"Thank you, Mr. Roper, I do not drink. I must admit I once knew you, but I must decline to renew the acquaintance."

"If you've come into some luck, you need not be so proud."

"Excuse me, I have an engagement," said Estcourt, looking at his watch, "at the Rose Club, of which I expect to be a member shortly."

"You a member!" echoed O'Kite.

"I think I said so."

"A member of our club!"

"That was the remark I had the honour to make. By the way, Mr. Macdermot O'Kite, I hear that the gentlemen who compose the Rose Club will subscribe £500 for you, if you will retire from it."

"Is it withdraw me name you mane?"

"Exactly."

"Be jabers, what will I do after such an insult."

"If you take my advice you'll hold on."

"Why?"

"You may get a thousand."

Saying this he bowed stiffly and went on, leaving the two friends paralysed with astonishment.

"Oh! by the kays of St. Pether," exclaimed the Macdermot O'Kite. "This is too much, carry me out and bury me dacently, for it's kilt intoirely I am."

"Wonders will never cease," said Roper. "I wish I had bitten my tongue out before I had spoken to him, but who would have expected this? I was never cut so dead in my life."

"He's got a fresh start."

"And he intends to keep it too."

"An' he givin' way to the liquor the way he did. Why he used to soak in it, so he did; how he's altered, he's got a white face; did you notice the nose av him? bedad, moin's a flaming baycon by the side av it. It's a regular sign for a dhoctor's shop, so it is; bad cess to it."

In high dudgeon they walked along, unable to reconcile themselves to the change in Vernon Estcourt's bearing and appearance generally.

Sir Lucius Holyoake was at the club, and saw Estcourt as soon as he sent in his card. He had known him in former days, but had lost sight of him during his period of decadence.

"My dear fellow!" he exclaimed, shaking him warmly by the hand; "I am so glad to see you. Where on earth have you been hiding all this time."

"Don't ask me," replied Estcourt. "I have been getting my bread somehow. Things are looking brighter, though, now."

"Well, what can I do for you? If I can be of service in any way, do not hesitate to command me."

"I thought I might serve you. Lately I have been acting as secretary to the member for Turnover."

"Tite Roper! The very man."

"Yes, I know," said Estcourt, quickly. "Certain facts have come to my knowledge of which I hold you ought to be put in possession. I am no Judas coming here to betray my master for so many pieces of silver, nor do I act altogether from a sense of duty. Roper, and his friend O'Kite, have grossly insulted me, and if I can do them any harm I will. That's how the matter stands."

"Thank you; if I only knew what money he has handled."

"I will tell you. Look at these papers," interrupted Estcourt.

Sir Lucius gladly consented to do so. They sat down together and went into the accounts, which plainly showed that Mr. Roper had misappropriated the funds of the club to the amount of several thousands. The result of this investigation was a stormy meeting when the committee met.

People wondered why Roper became suddenly indisposed, accepted the Chiltern Hundreds, and went to Boulogne for the benefit of his health. It was also a matter for surprise that O'Blatherem Macdermot O'Kite withdrew the Land Reclamation (Ireland) Bill, and was remarkably quiet during the remainder of the Session. Perhaps Vernon Estcourt knew; but he shortly afterwards proceeded to India, where he is occupying a good position in the Civil Service. Revenge is not an amiable passion, but it is sweet, and even the mildest mannered man feels like kicking back sometimes.

The *Patriot Flag* continues to electrify the people of Knockmadoon and neighbourhood with occasional outbursts of wrath, of which the following is a specimen, taken at random from its pages:—

"It is time," says the Macdermot O'Kite, "that Ireland threw off the grinding tyranny of the brutal Saxon, under the pressure of whose iron heel she has squirmed, and writhed, and groaned long enough. Let the Irish rise in their might. Every nation on earth wishes us success. The Powers stand aghast when they see the outrageous conduct of which we are the hapless victims. That foul and revolting rookery of corruption and misrule, the Castle, must go. It is doomed. Its days are numbered, and the sun is already dawning which is to usher in the glorious era of an Irish Republic. Stand shoulder to shoulder; let your hearts beat as one. The land grabbers are going; landlordism is tottering to its fate; and soon we shall be a united and independent nation. What can we think of a venal government that refused its support to the Knockmadoon Land Reclamation Company? They don't want any improvements. We are down, and they mean to keep us down by their alien soldiers and their mercenary bayonets, if they can. Our poverty is the opportunity of England; she dare not let us emerge from the slough of despond into which she has cast us. Therefore I say for the thousandth time, Rise and cast off this galling yoke which is making you the scorn and byword of the nations of the earth."

And so on, until the requisite amount of copy is ready for the printer, when the O'Kite gets into a cab and goes into the City to do a "put" or "call," or to speculate in some of these Foreign Stocks for which he had a predilection, and about which he was always flattering himself his position in the House gained him exclusive information, but which, if he had only known it, had been discounted long before he got within hail of Capel Court.

"Ah, bedad," he would murmur when the account went against him. "The City, sorr, is a sink of iniquity, so it is, and nothing better than a den of thaves. The men are ravenous wolves, saking whom they may devour, and a poor Irishman has no chance with the grasping Saxon at all, at all." And he would go back to Westminster by a penny steamboat.

But when his broker handed him a cheque he proceeded in high feather from the bank to a restaurant, where he indulged in a pint bottle of champagne all alone, and, swelling like the frog in the fable, said to himself "London is the City against the world. It's full of money. I would not live in any other for a pension. Its merchants and its brokers are the illigant gintlemen. What's Paris, Vienna, or New York? It's a pound to a postage stamp London wins all the time." And, lighting a cigar, the Macdermot O'Kite would proudly hail a hansom and shout to the driver in the ears of an admiring crowd, "To the House of Commons wid yees Mimbers' entrance, do ye moind now."

THE HYPOCHONDRIAC,

OR

A CURE FOR THE BLUES.

THE HYPOCHONDRIAC,

OR

A CURE FOR THE BLUES.

PRETTY Kate Benson was called the sunbeam of the house, and she was fully entitled to the description. When her father and mother died, her uncle, Sir William Benson, Bart., K.S.I., adopted her, and from the time she was sixteen until she was twenty-one, at which period we introduce her to the reader, she had made sunshine for him. Sir William was a bachelor, verging upon fifty years of age, who had held a Civil appointment in India, retiring from the service with a handsome fortune and a pension, two things very conducive to long life and happiness. He kept house in a quiet street near Portman Square, and Kate was his housekeeper and factotum. Very fond was he of his pretty, dark-haired niece, who flitted about like a fairy, and sang as merrily as a bird in spring-time. Kate was beloved by all who knew her, and he had set his mind on her making a grand match. In his opinion, she was fit to be a duchess. He had her presented at Court by the Countess of Camellburg, and gave parties in her honour to a distinguished circle. Many were her suitors among members of the liberal professions, representatives of the peerage, and the diplomatic corps. She was affable to the highest and the lowest, though her moods were variable, for she could snub a duke as neatly as she could put a flower in her uncle's coat. But, strange to say, none found favour in her eyes. Not that Kate was cold, fastidious, or proud. A warmer-hearted girl never lived.

She was very attentive to her religious duties; taught in a Sunday-school, and visited the poor in their homes, giving away in pure unostentatious charity more than even her intimate friends had any idea of. One of her favourite methods of slumming was to visit pawnbrokers' shops in low neighbourhoods, and ask the proprietors to point out those whom they deemed worthy of assistance. Many a poor woman, who had vainly tried to borrow an extra sixpence on a threadbare quilt to buy bread or firing for her children, was made happy by the unexpected gift of a few shillings from Kate's charitable hand. Her philosopher and guide, in this kind of work, was the Reverend John Fentyman, curate of the parish, an Oxford man, a gentleman, and a true Christian. He was handsome, eloquent, very High-Church, somewhat pale and thin for a man of six-and-twenty, which might be accounted for by his austerity, and he was rendered peculiarly interesting by an hereditary tendency to consumption. What more did a romantic girl want to fall in love with? Kate Benson surrendered her heart to John Fentyman, without his so much as asking for it, and that was why lords and excellencies were neglected. Sir William took no more notice of the reverend gentleman than if he had been an upper servant. The idea of Kate—his pretty, pampered, spoilt, petted Kate—throwing herself away on a poor curate, never entered his head. If it had done, he would have dismissed it as being too absurd. But the seed was sown, and the harvest was ready for reaping, before he had the least inkling of it. He was like a man living on volcanic soil. An eruption might take place at any time, which would scatter his ambitious hopes like chaff before the wind. Fentyman was an honourable man; he loved Kate, and the unspoken language that existed between lovers told him that his affection was returned a hundredfold; but he had not said one word to her about his feelings. That Sir William might object, and probably would, to an alliance between him and his niece, he more than suspected. What was his duty under the circumstances? There could be only one course for him to pursue, and that was to unburden his mind to Sir William, and ask his permission to pay his addresses to his niece. This he did, not without certain misgivings, fearing, trembling, and being greatly exercised in his mind. It was early on a May morning when he called. Time was valuable with him. He had to visit a soup-kitchen at twelve, to arrange about penny dinners for Board School children; at two he had to attend a foreign Bible mission at Exeter Hall; at four there was an examination in the church of aspirants for confirmation; in fact, he seldom had an hour to himself, wherein to smoke the seductive pipe, which was the only vice he indulged in. Sir William received him in the morning-room, putting down his paper as he entered. It was generally a matter of business when the reverend gentleman called.

"Oh," thought Sir William, "a subscription, I suppose. These fellows are always begging!"

"Sit down, Mr. Fentyman. I wish you good-morning. It is a fine day!" exclaimed the baronet, conventionally.

"Ahem!" coughed the curate, which was a habit, the excitement under which he was labouring did not prompt him to check. "The weather is remarkably fine, Sir William. Under Providence, I trust we shall have a good harvest."

"Yes, I shouldn't wonder, Anything new?"

"Nothing new, Sir William."

The baronet yawned, and looked out of the window. He was quite prepared to hear that the aborigines of the Fiji Islands wanted some new pyjamas, and was equally prepared to say, in stereotyped phrase, "Put me down for a guinea, Mr. Fentyman. I would give more willingly, but really I have so many demands upon my purse, you know," &c.

The curate felt the silence awkward. The burden fell upon him. If the Islanders had wanted anything, he could have pleaded their cause glibly enough. But it was for himself that he had to plead, and that for which he was about to ask was something so precious that his breath was almost taken away when he thought of his presumption. It was like taking a plunge into a cold bath on a winter's morning, or having a tooth out. However, it had to be done, and with a brief silent prayer for help he took the header.

"Sir William," he said, "I want to speak to you about your niece."

Kate was at that moment in the region of the kitchen, looking over the contents of the larder, and giving orders for dinner, for she prided herself on being useful as well as ornamental.

"Hasn't she been punctual in her attendance at church lately?" asked the baronet.

"Oh, yes, no young lady could be more diligent in her religious duties."

"What is the matter, then?"

In preaching a sermon to a thousand people Fentyman would not have faltered, but in this instance he felt a coward.

"Ahem! the fact is," he rejoined, "I—that is—what's your opinion, Sir William, of Shelley as a poet?"

He had come within an ace of the point, but he had not the courage to speak out. It was a case of the thoroughbred steeplechaser refusing the water-jump when on the brink. He shied unmistakably, and though he metaphorically dug the spurs into himself, he could not face it.

"I never read poetry," replied the baronet, curtly.

"His 'Ode to a Skylark' is a gem; it is unique, like Tennyson's 'Mariana in the moated Grange,'" continued the reverend gentleman, hopelessly floundering about in the mire of his own creating.

"What has that got to do with my niece, sir?"

"Your niece, Sir William—ahem!"

"Yes, my niece, sir."

"I—I—ahem! I came to ask your kind permission to pay my addresses to her."

It was out now. The deed was done; but it is a question whether it could have been done more clumsily.

Sir William bent an inexorable glance upon him, which ought to have withered him if he had seen it, but he did not, for the good and sufficient reason that he was studying the rather complex pattern of the carpet, and wishing that the floor would open, and let him through into the vestry of the church, where he would be more at home, or that he was a thousand miles at sea, or some other equally impossible thing, and he hummed to himself the words of the old song, "Oh, would I were a bird," but he was a long way off from having wings as yet.

"The devil, you did!" ejaculated Sir William.

"Don't—don't swear," said the curate.

"D—— it! sir. I can't help it; you make me."

"Pray be calm. Consider the proprieties."

"Bother the proprieties. Have you spoken to Miss Benson about this—this unhappy attachment of yours?"

"Not a word."

"Then mind you don't. Leave this house at once, Mr. Fentyman, and never come into it again," said Sir William, with suppressed fury. "I respect your cloth, but, by the living Jingo——"

"Don't, Sir William, pray, pray don't."

"I shan't be able to keep my hands off you, if I hear of this again."

"Then you refuse?"

"Flatly—absolutely. Good day."

Sir William held the door open, and tapped sullenly on the floor with his foot.

"Is there no hope, Sir William?"

"None. Good-day."

Mr. Fentyman gathered up his hat and umbrella. He turned very red, and then very white; he coughed twice, and he took his departure with a respectful bow.

Sir William watched him out of the front door.

"Gone!" he said. "It was tempting, but I'm glad I did not kick him. Wants my niece, eh? What next, d—— his impudence."

His bronzed face, tanned by an Indian sun, lighted up with a glow of honest indignation. He did not say a word about the audacious proposal to Kate. An hour afterwards their horses came to the door, and they went for a canter in the park. In the Row they met the old Duke of Fitzfaddle, who had £30,000 a year and the gout. Kate and he indulged in a flirtation, and Sir William smiled as he thought something might come of it. He would have liked Fitzfaddle for a son-in-law; there wasn't a man at the Oriental Club who could play a better game at whist, and he had some old port and priceless Madeira in his cellar that was a treat.

Weeks went on, and Kate Benson did not become engaged;

she had several advantageous offers, all of which she refused. In short, suitors fell before her like leaves in Vallambrose. The men could not make her out, she was indifferent alike to young and old, rich and poor.

At last the secret came out.

Sir William descended to breakfast as usual, but Kate was not there. He found a letter on his plate in her handwriting; the paper was blotted with tears, as if it had cost her an effort to write it; at all events, it cost her uncle an effort to read it. His eyes swam, his brain grew dizzy, and he breathed with difficulty as he mastered its startling contents, which were as follows :—

"Dearest and best of relatives, my more than father. How shall I break the news to you? I fear you will call me a sinful wretch, and never speak to me again ; but I was forced to obey the dictates of my heart. I can scarcely hope for your forgiveness. How could I do it, after all your kindness to me? I can scarcely write the words. John loved me, and I loved him. He would have fled from me, as in honour bound ; I could not hear of it. Yesterday we were married. This morning I leave your house. God help you to bear the shock. John has accepted a curacy at the East End of London. We shall be out of your sight. If you can forgive us, a line to us at St. Jude's, Limehouse, will bring me at once to your side. Be merciful, do not judge me too harshly. All the happiness of my future life is bound up in my husband. I felt I could not tell a falsehood at the altar. Wealth did not dazzle me ; poverty has no terrors for me. I can assure you, my dear uncle, that for some time past I have been nearly distracted between the duty I owed to you and the love I feel for my husband. I cannot reconcile the step I have taken with my conscience, in fact I can't argue myself in the right at all. I can only throw myself on your mercy I will ever pray that you may not feel my loss greatly. If you can have us by your side, say so. If I do not hear from you, I shall know that I have committed an unpardonable sin in your eyes, and am discarded. It will be hard to bear, but I will try, with God's help, to bear up. My heart is full of affection for you. I may have been weak, but I have every reason to be proud of my husband.

Do not curse me, dear uncle. Try to think kindly of one whom you were fond of calling your little girl, KATE."

This letter explained itself. Kate had secretly married Mr. Fentyman, and left her uncle's luxurious home to live the life of the wife of a poor curate at the East End of London. Infatuated with her love, she had been blind to the consequences of her act. Sir William's face grew very stern and grave as he crumpled up the letter and threw it into the fireplace. He considered that he had been treated with the basest ingratitude. The blow was a keen one, and he felt it as much as if she had been his own daughter. Never would he forgive her. Neither she nor Fentyman should darken his doors. That was his resolution. Summoning the servants, he announced the fact of his niece's marriage; gave them notice to leave in a month, saying that he was about to travel; and proceeding to a house agent arranged for the sale of his furniture and effects. The house was hateful to him now that Kate was gone; he had no use for it. Never would he give another party. He feared he would be an object of ridicule to his friends, or, worse still, of sympathy, so he decided on Paris as his future place of residence. It was nearly twelve o'clock when he had done all this. His breakfast had been untasted. Finding himself close to Hanover Square, he determined to drop in at his club and have something to eat, as his head felt rather weak. When crossing George Street, he did not see a hansom cab which was coming along at a quick pace.

"Hi! hi!" cried the driver.

He was thinking of Kate, and did not imagine that the warning was addressed to him.

"Look out! Hi!" exclaimed people on the pavement.

Still he paid no attention.

The next moment he was knocked down by the horse, which seemed to have a dozen legs all treading on him at once. Then all was a blank, until he came to himself in the accident ward of St. Mary's Hospital, Paddington, whither the police had taken him. No bone was broken, but he had received a severe shock to the system, and the house surgeon said there was a slight concussion of the brain. He recovered sufficiently to give his name, and the evening papers contained a brief account of the affair, as follows:—

"*Accident to Sir William Benson.*—As Sir William Benson, Bart., was crossing George Street. Hanover Square, at noon to-day, he was knocked down and run over by a hansom cab. He was at once conveyed to St. Mary's Hospital, but we are glad to learn that the injuries he has received are not considered serious, though they may occasion his detention at the hospital for some days."

Kate saw this in the paper, and was much concerned. Without mentioning her intention to her husband, she hastened to St. Mary's and requested to see the sufferer. Her presence was notified to Sir William, who firmly refused to either see or speak to her. So Kate went away heartbroken, knowing that there was no forgiveness for her. She had got her answer: he was implacable; there was no free pardon to be expected, and she resigned herself to her fate. It added to the poignancy of her regret however. She blamed herself for the accident. If Sir William had not been upset by her departure, the chances were that he would have kept his eyes open and not have been run over. As time went on she found she could not undo what she had done. It is a painful necessity in this world that as we make our beds we must lie on them, and she had to live her life. What was it? The humdrum life of a poor curate's wife, which, as a matter of dry fact, was very different to what she had expected.

Week followed week with unvarying monotony, and her experience was very bitter. The rose-coloured dreams of her girlhood were not realized. There was all the difference between romance and reality.

The lodgings she occupied were cheap, of course, and not nice. The people her husband and she had to labour amongst were the reverse of agreeable. Never had she dreamed of so much vice, debauchery and hypocrisy It was a trouble to make both ends meet. Not being brought up economically she did not know how to manage her slender income properly. She got into debt with tradespeople, and was horribly dunned in consequence. To dress, in the proper sense of the word, was impossible; she could only clothe herself. Fentyman was very kind to her, but he was out a great deal, and she found herself lonely. By degrees it began to dawn upon Kate that her marriage was a mistake. Fentyman's cough developed itself, and she had to nurse him. Instead of enjoying halcyon days, she grew miserable, and longed once more for the home her uncle had given her. Then she had horses, carriages, dresses, delicacies for the table, money to spend as she liked. Now—but why pursue the contrast further? She found that she had made a fool of herself, and her husband's love did not compensate for what she had lost. It was a bitter confession, but there was no help for it. Yet, like a true and loving wife, she concealed her real sentiments from Fentyman, who went on the even tenor of his way, and saw nothing odd in his wife's pale face, absent manner, and red eyes.

If she underwent an alteration, so did Sir William. When he left the hospital he went into lodgings. His orders as to breaking up his establishment and selling off had been carried out to the letter. His former friends found him morose and unsociable; he was always grumbling; nothing gave him pleasure; he took a pessimist view of everything. Formerly he had been gay and jocund, and would crack the merry jest with any one. He had been full of anecdotes, as most old Indians are, and had as large a budget as any competition wallah had ever been blessed with. But now he seldom told any stories, and scarcely took the trouble to listen if he was addressed by one in the story-telling vein. In fact, he was a confirmed hypochondriac of the worst and most pronounced type. He began to think he was the chosen seat of disease, and proved a small fortune to patent medicine sellers, whose nostrums he bought in a reckless manner. He abused every Prime Minister, from Lord Melbourne to Lord Aberdeen, and from Lord John Russell, to Disraeli and Gladstone. All his acquaintances noticed and regretted the change in him. Even the crossing sweeper in the square near the club felt it. He used to receive a penny; now he only got sworn at if he touched his broken-rimmed hat as of old. He took the avocation of the ladies out of their hands, and squabbled with cabmen over an extra shilling, and was a perfect terror to the waiters at his club, who found it impossible to please him. He never could get a sufficient supply of bread; he had been known to eat a dozen pieces, and his loud voice was incessantly heard shouting, "Bread!" This state of mind did not make him a pleasant companion, and he soon got himself disliked. Only one friend adhered to him. This was Captain Charteris—a man about his own age—who had known him in India. He had once done Charteris a kindness which he could not forget. At a critical time he had lent the captain some money, which had saved him the loss of his commission, and through good and evil report Charteris was always his friend. They lodged in the same street, and were much together. It was hard to bear Sir William's ill temper, but Charteris did so somehow. He knew all about Kate's marriage, and how her desertion had affected her uncle; but even he did not dare to hint at a reconciliation more than once. When he had done so, Sir William flew in a terrible passion and taking up the poker broke everything he could in the room. Her name was never mentioned, and it was understood that it was to be tabooed. So the months flew by, and the baronet's temper did not improve. He could not find a cure for the blues. One morning the postman brought him a letter. Captain Charteris was breakfasting with him. When Sir William had read it, he handed it to the captain with a grim smile of intense satisfaction, in which hatred and uncharitableness struggled for the mastery.

"Read that," he cried, in a voice of triumph. "Somebody's chickens have come home to roost. Serves the hussy right for her ingratitude, and Fentyman too. Bah! how I hate the name. Read it aloud. Let me hear it."

It was from Kate, who said, "My dear Uncle,—You will be surprised at hearing from poor little me. I am nearly broken-hearted."

"Never thought of my heart," ejaculated Sir William.

"Heaven blessed me with a dear baby; but alas! it only lived long enough for me to learn to love it. Then it was taken away We buried it to-day."

"Good job too. Can't keep themselves, I'll warrant," Sir William interjected. "I wish it had been twins. I've heard of happiness being born a twin, and I don't see why misery should not be."

"We had intended to christen it after you."

"After—a long way after—not before me," ejaculated Sir William.

"I can hardly write for crying. My troubles seem more than I can bear. John is seriously ill. His cough has become chronic, and the doctor says his chest is affected——"

"Chest! His money chest, I suppose," said Sir William, with a ghastly attempt at a pun.

"Which I thought all along was the case. It is a hacking cough, which keeps him and me awake at night."

"Shouldn't have had him. Might have known he was consumptive. Go on. Ha! ha! He'll never die of yellow fever. My gold won't affect him."

"Now I come to the most difficult part of my letter. John's income is so small, and he works so hard for so little. We are in debt, which is a dreadful thing for a clergyman. Doctor's bills run up so, and medicines are very dear. He requires strengthening, and I have to buy him port wine and things. Do you think you could find it in your heart to spare us a little money?"

"Not a shilling!" cried Sir William. "Nobody ever paid for my port wine."

"You didn't want it," remarked Charteris.

"Who said I did?"

"No one. But——"

"Go on with the letter, sir."

"If it was ever so little it would be a help. John is writing a book. It is a Life of the Apostle Paul, and if he sells it he will be sure to repay you."

"It's been done to death. Everybody has had a go in at Paul, from Renan downward. Won't sell. If he was alive now his whole body wouldn't fetch a pound."

Though somewhat disconcerted by Sir William's interruption, Captain Charteris continued to read on to the end, like the Good Samaritan he was; but if he hoped to move the baronet's flinty heart, he was mistaken. As for himself, his resources were strictly limited. He had enough to live upon, and that was all. Consequently he could do nothing for the curate's wife. He had the will, but not the means. He went on with the letter:

"I scarcely like to ask you, but necessity has no law. Will you generously forget the past, and come to our aid? John knows nothing of this application. If he did, it is doubtful if he would let it go."

"Humbug," snapped Sir William. "He was looking over her shoulder all the time she was writing."

"How do you know?" asked Charteris.

"He prompted her about the port wine. Don't tell me?"

"I was dear to you once. Be brave, be kind, be good, and Heaven will reward you.—KATE."

"It won't do. I'm not to be smoothed over in that way." said Sir William, shaking his head. "She has only herself to blame."

"Shall I answer it?" asked the Captain.

"If you do, I will never speak to you again. Put it in another envelope, and send it back to the address. They may starve, for what I care."

His wishes were at once complied with, and that episode was ended. Poor Kate, how eagerly she was watching for the postman. It was cruel, but she had brought it on herself. One thing Captain Charteris did, which reflected credit on his head and heart. Unobserved he made a note in his pocketbook of the address, if at any future time Sir William should relent, and want to know where his niece lived. Nevertheless his severity was a great deal assumed. When he got up to go out soon afterwards, he blew his nose and rubbed his eyes. He was deeply affected, but his obstinate disposition would not allow him to give in. In the passage he passed the housemaid, who saw a change in him at once.

"What ever is the matter with Sir William?" she muttered; "he looks five years older."

Sir William had an appointment that morning to go to Captain Charteris' apartments for a particular purpose. The Captain had a taste for painting in oils. If the truth must be told, he was an execrably bad artist. The dealers fought shy of him, and it is needless to say that the Academy and the Grosvenor Gallery knew him not. His studio contained several unsaleable works of art, but he had just completed one which, to encourage him, Sir William had promised to buy, if he liked it, for the sum of £100, though its probable value was £20, and it would have been dear at that. Already it had gone through several alterations and modifications. Originally it had been called "Pharaoh Crossing the Red Sea," but Sir William objected to the Egyptian ruler, so it was changed into "The Battle of Trafalgar." The chariots became ships, the horsemen sailors, and the king was metamorphosed into Nelson. This day was fixed for an inspection of the canvas, and after breakfast they adjourned to the studio, where the painting was resting on the easel.

Sir William Benson was in the mood of a captious critic, and would have picked holes in the Madonna di San Sisto and quarrelled with Raphael about his chiaoscuro. The letter with which Kate had favoured him had not tended to allay his irritabilty, and he was eager and ready to find fault.

"What do you want for that?" he inquired.

"Oh, I leave that to you," replied the artist.

"You English artists charge by the yard."

Posing before the picture, he took a long look, and his face lighted up with an intelligent scorn.

Captain Charteris saw the storm coming, and said, "Well, what do you think of it?"

"It's a daub, sir," replied the baronet, "I wouldn't hang it in my kitchen."

"Why not? may I ask."

"That leading figure is no more like Nelson than its predecessor was like Pharaoh."

"I flatter myself that is a very good Nelson."

"Bah! Did Nelson have two arms at the Battle of Trafalgar? let me ask you that."

This criticism was a poser; unfortunately the captain had forgotten all about the one arm and the one eye of the great naval hero, and had made him a perfect man. There he was with two arms and a couple of eyes. It was very annoying, but there was no getting over it.

"I really forgot," he stammered. "But if Nelson was only half a man, he was all a hero."

"An artist, sir, let me tell you, should never forget; he

must always be true to nature," continued the hypercritical baronet; "and let me tell you, that your waves are more like mountains than anything else; that foam which caps them is suggestive of snow on the many-peaked summit of the Rigi. No, it won't do at all."

Captain Charteris was in despair.

He had dethroned Pharaoh to please his difficult patron, and Nelson reigned in his stead, without any avail.

"What shall I do with it?" he queried, sadly.

"Burn it, I should say, there is not colour enough."

"I'll alter it again with pleasure."

"No you won't. No man ever took a pleasure in altering his own work; you will alter it to please me, but not with pleasure. Now I should advise you to drop all idea of Nelson; you are not cut out for a marine painter; make it Hannibal crossing the Alps."

"Good gracious!" cried the captain.

"Nelson, with a little alteration, will do very well for Hannibal, and you have your mountains cut and dried for you."

"But the ships, my dear Sir William?"

"Turn them into baggage wagons."

"Horrible! I mean, it is doubtful if they had any."

"Perhaps you will tell me that so astute a captain as Hannibal proved himself to be, wandered hundreds of miles from his base without any commissariat."

"Well, I'll make it Hannibal, or the Gods on Mount Olympus, or the King of the Cannibal Islands, if you like, with Hokey Pokey in the middle: but I should like to be paid for what I have done; colours cost money, and there is a lot of colouring in that picture."

"I'll give it you," replied Sir William, "if I thought you were going to buy siennas and sepias and chromes, but you are not."

"What then?"

"I know," said the baronet, with an artful look, "you want to get some money out of me to take to that jade Kate, and say it comes from me."

The captain could not deny this; he looked the guilty wretch he was, his soft-hearted plan had been seen through, and his charitable intention frustrated. Kate's letter was haunting his mind; he pictured her in her miserable Eastend lodging in some slum, moaning over her dead baby boy, and shivering with a nameless dread every time she heard her husband's hacking cough.

"Never mind," replied the captain, taking up his brush and aiming a savage blow at Nelson's face, which entirely obliterated the features of that distinguished individual.

"What did you do that for?" exclaimed Sir William, "he'd have made a good Hannibal."

"How the deuce," asked Charteris, losing his temper, "can a Carthaginian resemble an Englishman?"

"You should write the names underneath."

"Oh, yes, I daresay; perhaps I don't know the difference between a Christian admiral and a heathen general."

"I'll bet you can't tell what kind of a uniform Hannibal wore."

"I don't know, and what's more I don't care."

"That's where it is; you'll never be an artist, because you won't take pains. You're only fit for a scene painter's assistant in a transpontine theatre."

The altercation was assuming an acrimonious character, as if often did between these two, in spite of the captain's pliable temper, when it was interrupted by the appearance of a mutual friend in the person of Mr. St. Albans Smith, who had been invited to view the picture. Mr. Smith was spoken of as something in the City; nobody knew exactly what he did, but as a matter of fact he was a speculator on the Stock Exchange, spending his time all the year round at his broker's office. A very shrewd man was St. Albans Smith; he knew the value and prospects of every stock in the market. After shaking hands, he looked at the battle-piece, and shook his head.

"Too much colour," he remarked.

"Sir William thinks there is not colour enough," replied Charteris. "But then nothing pleases him."

"Is that true?" asked St. Albans Smith.

"Yes, I'll admit it," answered the baronet, frankly. "I'm soured, my liver has gone wrong. Ever since my niece threw herself away on a poor curate named Fentyman

K

—bah! how I hate the name, and I got run over by a cab I've been an altered man."

"Do you object to the curate because he is poor?"

"Partly."

"That is easily remedied. Get him made a bishop. You have plenty of interest; hunt up your friends. As to the liver part of the question, you want excitement."

"Oh, I get plenty of that, something is always worrying me into a fever."

"Come with me into the City to-morrow, I'll wake you up."

"How?"

"I'll take you to my brokers. You shall have a tape all to yourself, and speculate to your heart's content, making five-pound notes by the minute."

"What's a tape? I don't understand it," said Sir William.

"You soon will. Shall I call for you to-morrow morning? I'll undertake your noviciate—you shall be entered apprentice, fellow-craft, and master-mason, as it were, all in a day. Is it an appoinment?"

"Do you think it would dissipate this gloom that oppresses me?"

"Finest cure going for the blues!"

"And remove my irritability?" Sir William went on.

"Undoubtedly—try it!" said St. Albans Smith. "It's more exciting than card-playing, or betting on horse-races, and more profitable, if you pay it proper attention."

"I'll come! The rivers of Damascus have done me no good, and I'll try your Jordan," said Sir William.

"You won't regret it. I say, Charteris, what *do* you call that conglomeration of red and white in the corner?"

"It's the setting sun," answered the captain.

"'Pon my word, it looks like eggs-and-bacon. Turner isn't in it with you!"

"How would you have the sun set?"

"Decently, of course, not like a pot of melted butter struck by lightning; don't let anybody else see it. You are clever, but genius is no excuse for a thing like that!"

"That's what I tell him," said the baronet, "and he kicks like a mule: did you ever see such ships?"

"They are better than the waves—it's a kind of sea gone mad!" replied Smith.

Captain Charteris groaned.

"I shall go mad, if you don't leave off!" he exclaimed.

"Tone it down!" responded Smith.

"Touch it up!" said Sir William.

Driven desperate, the artist dabbed his brush on his palette, and, raking up some Prussian blue, attacked the unhappy canvas furiously, soon obliterating every vestige of the sea-fight.

"There!—will that please you?" he demanded.

"That's it—now you've got your ground-work to go upon;" answered Sir William. "Fleck your blue a little with white, and you have your Alpine cloud-land—stick in!"

He looked round—the captain had vanished.

"Hullo!—where has the beggar gone?" he cried.

"He's off, as the fly said when he got out of the mustard pot!" rejoined St. Albans Smith. "That's what my friend Langford always says, when the spirit moves him."

"Who's Langford?"

"The broker I'm going to take you to; don't forget. I must run—my Trunks want looking after!"

"Trunks—are you going a journey?"

"Ha—ha! It's a Canadian railway stock. Ta, ta!—to-morrow I cure your fit of the blues!"

St. Albans Smith hurried away, and, finding himself alone, the baronet returned to his own lodgings, to indulge in a wrangle with his landlady about her weekly bill, in which he thought she had charged him too much for coals.

He saw no more of the artist that day, but when Captain Charteris called upon Sir William Benson next day in Seymour Street he found the baronet pacing the room on the ground floor, which he occupied as a parlour, fuming and fretting, and looking the picture of misery and despair. At the time he was ushered in Sir William stopped at the window, shaking his fist at some object in the street. What that was it was not difficult to discover, as an organ-grinder exactly opposite was playing some sort of a lively jig, to the inspiriting tune of which sundry ragged unkempt urchins were dancing *pede libero*. Charteris, with his smiling face and gay air, presented a striking contrast to his morose and grumbling friend, who had ceased to find any delight in living.

"Hullo! what's the matter now?" he asked. "Has your banker suspended payment, or the only girl you ever loved run away with a market gardener?"

"Confound it!" replied Sir William, swinging round in his loose cashmere dressing-gown; "everything seems to go against me. I don't know how it is, but hang it all, my life is a perpetual torment. Excuse my abruptness; take a chair. How are you?"

"Excellent well," said Captain Charteris. "What is the trouble at this particular moment?"

"That organ-grinder, d—, I mean bless him, with a prodigiously big, big B."

He could tolerate the old organs better than the new ones; they gave you a tune which lasted a quarter of an hour. The new ones changed too quickly for him. He was no sooner tortured by the "Sweet by and by" than he was maddened by "Darling, I am growing old," and when this was corkscrewed into his aching head his throbbing brain was gimletted by "Wait till the clouds roll by."

"Move him on."

"He won't move. I offered him twopence, but he says he never moves on under fourpence, and of course my old fool of a landlady can't find a policeman."

"Never can, my dear fellow, when he's wanted. The attraction of unlimited mutton pie in some area is too strong."

Sir William grated his teeth together savagely.

"Oh!" he groaned, "how I should like to kill an organ-grinder."

"Don't," replied Captain Charteris, "you would be hanged."

"All the better."

"Eh?"

"It would be a happy release."

"Wait for an experienced hangman," said Charteris.

"One is as good as another."

"No, every generation does not produce its Calcraft; you wouldn't like to be bungled over?"

"What's the odds?"

"Pause," said the captain, laughing. "The penalty exacted by stern unrelenting justice is painful, the surroundings are horrid. Did you ever see a man hanged?"

"No, but I should like to see a dozen I know served that way," snapped Sir William.

"I have. The chaplain precedes the tottering pinioned wretch, who, limp as a rag, is supported by warders on each side, while the chaplain reads the burial service. The prison bell goes 'boom!' striking a knell to the doomed man's heart. It's horrible."

"Go on," said Sir William.

"Eh?"

"I like that. It's better than Young's 'Night Thoughts,' or Harvey's 'Meditations among the Tombs,' or 'The Castle of Otranto.'"

"You are a cheerful companion."

"I assure you I haven't enjoyed anything so much, since I was in the Catacombs at Rome. Go on."

"If I were you, I'd take lodgings over an undertaker's shop; when they are executing an order for coffins at night, the hammering would be highly agreeable, I should say."

"Not a bad idea, but do go on."

"It is easily pictured, this last quarter of an hour of a condemned man's life. First the chaplain saying, in a dull chant, 'I am the resurrection and the life,' then the bell, 'boom,' so on until the scaffold is reached, then, mounting the steps, the horrible precision with which the rope is adjusted, 'boom' again, and—dash it, I can't go on. I shall have a fit of the blues myself if I do; pandering to the cravings of a misanthrope like you, is worse than holding a brief for the devil."

"Thank you. I like to be insulted in my own house," said Sir William, sarcastically.

"Really you are unbearable."

"You can go. I shall appreciate your room as well as your company."

This rude speech caused Captain Charteris to take his hat in his hand.

"I am going, Benson," he exclaimed, "and when I darken your door again you can tell me of it."

With this he hastened from the room, leaving the baronet all alone in the dumps.

"There," he said, "I've done it. The fool's gone. I didn't think he meant it. Now I've lost my only friend; and just as he got on conversation I liked. I was waiting for him to describe the body after death."

He felt more thoroughly miserable than he had ever done before.

"If I had a pistol, upon my soul I think I'd put an end to myself. What use am I? I'm not only a curse to myself but to everybody else with my vile temper. All alone now; that's a nice look out. I shall have to ride outside 'busses, and spend a small fortune in treating the drivers for the sake of getting some one to talk to."

Again he paced the room impatiently.

"All alone," he muttered, "all alone."

He did not know how necessary Captain Charteris had been to his existence until he had lost him.

He was not quite alone, however, for the next minute St. Albans Smith drove up in a cab, and Sir William gladly recollected his promise to take him into the city.

"Have I kept you waiting?" asked Mr. Smith, as he entered.

As a matter of fact he had not, for the baronet had forgotten all about the engagement, but his grumbling, fault-finding disposition would not allow him to reply graciously.

"Yes, you have, and I don't like it," he answered. "It is a very ungentlemanly thing to do."

"I apologize."

"So you ought. I'm not accustomed to be treated in this way."

"It shan't occur again."

"No. I'll take jolly good care it shan't," said Sir William, becoming all the more bullying and snappish as the other gave way to him.

St. Albans Smith smiled.

"Oh! you dear old bear," he exclaimed.

"Eh! What?" growled the baronet.

"What a treat you are; but we'll soon cure all that. If I were a collector of rare specimens I'd have such a fossilised antediluvian stuffed and put in a glass case."

"Stuff me?"

"Most decidedly."

"Put me in a glass case?"

"Why not?"

"Sir," cried Sir William, "you've called me a fossil, antediluvian, and a bear. I demand an explanation, a satisfaction, a reparation, sir."

"Oh! yes. That's all right; take it. I'll send it you in writing when I get home, so that there shall be no mistake, and you can have it framed and hang it over the mantelpiece. Or keep my signature by you; it will be useful if you want to commit forgery at any time, don't you know," rejoined St. Albans Smith "But I say, Benson, old fellow——"

"Don't be so plaguy familiar, sir."

"I understand your malady, and mean to cure it. But which are you going to be to-day, a 'bear' or a 'bull'?"

"If you call me any more names——"

"Do be quiet and listen to me, Diogenes the Second. Come out of your tub for once. Put that stick down," he added, as Sir William threatened him with an assegai that had been presented to him by a chief on the African "continong."

"My blood is boiling, sir, at these repeated insults."

"Let it simmer down. Now I'll explain. We are all 'bulls' or 'bears' on the Stock Exchange, operating against one another, as it were; the 'bulls' for a rise, the 'bears' for a fall. You give your broker, say, £10, which is the lowest amount, and for the time you are the holder of 1,000 stock. You sit near the tape and watch the prices as they are telegraphed to the office from the 'House,' where the jobbers make the prices according to the way business goes."

"Humph! that's it," replied Sir William. "I don't think I shall care for it."

"I should be a 'bull' to-day of Brighton A's, Unified, Mex. Rails, and Grand Trunks, or a 'bear' of Districts, Chathams, and Russian. Come and join me."

" In all of those ? "

" Not all. Take one to begin with, say, Brighton A's; the weather's beautiful, the dividend is expected to be a good one, and the traffic return is better. See my idea ? "

" Yes," replied Sir William. " Do you operate largely ? "

" Sometimes. I 'beared' 20,000 Suez Canals from par to 30, and made 70 per cent., or £700 on a £10 cover."

" Indeed. Suppose your judgment is wrong ? "

" I never follow a stock too far. I always cut losses."

" Excuse my ebullition of wrath just now," said Sir William.

" Don't mention it. Abuse me again if you like as we go along in the cab."

Greatly mollified, Sir William accompanied his friend to Mr. Langford's offices, when he was duly introduced to the broker and several of the *habitués* of the place. He made his investment as directed, and took up a position near a tape, of which there were several.

He got into Brighton A's at 105½, buying 5,000 stock, and waited.

It was early, twelve o'clock having only just struck, and the market was firm. Eagerly Sir William watched the tape as it rolled out into the basket, being as pleased as a child with a new toy. It told him that Consols were 95½ for money, and presently he read Brighton 106¼.

Prices were going in his favour. He forgot all about his troubles.

His excitement became intense. St. Albans Smith had gone out to have a glass of wine. It was a weakness of his to pop out and have a glass of wine very frequently.

" How goes it ? " he asked of his *protégé*.

" Capitally," replied the baronet. " This machine is a splendid invention."

Click ! click !

" It's at it again," he added.

" Consols," read Smith aloud, " 95¼ ⅜. Just the way I want the markets to go. Brighton 137 to ¼ ; Districts 36¾."

" What shall I do ? " asked Sir William.

" Take your profits. You've made 1½ on Brightons—that's £75, and that in less than an hour. How do you like it ? "

"First rate."

"Feel better?" asked Smith.

"Rather! Have I really made £75?"

"Certainly."

"Can I take it?"

"Whenever you like, my dear fellow."

"Can I have my cheque?" continued Sir William, pleased, but somewhat confused.

"Haven't I told you so? In this office they always pay promptly. I will attend to it for you."

Sir William smiled childishly, while Smith asked the manager to close the account for the new client and make out his cheque.

Presently a cheque for the amount he had made was handed to Sir William.

"Come and have a bit of lunch somewhere," he said.

"With pleasure," replied St. Albans Smith.

Sir William was actually thawing. His icy demeanour was melting beneath the genial influence of the tape. Not since his accident had he been known to ask anyone to have so much as a cigar.

As they were going out of the office, Mr. Langford came in.

"Well, Sir William," he said in a cheery tone. "How are your Brighton A's?"

"Couldn't be better," replied the baronet.

"That's all right."

"I shall come back again directly and do something else."

"Whatever you like."

Sir William's face wore a smile. In the passage a dog got under his feet. For a wonder he did not kick it.

"Poor dog!" he was actually heard to remark.

At lunch he laughed, and seemed to enjoy what he ate; the atmosphere of the city gave him an appetite; he spoke well of Mr. Langford, and said he liked the people he had met at the office. In the afternoon he was again at his post near the tape he had first selected, and did a little in Unified and Turkish, the result being satisfactory.

During the remainder of the week he was every day at

Mr. Langford's office, and he became a changed man ; he made many friends. No longer selfish and churlish, he had a pleasant word for everybody. Of course his judgment was not always right, but he had discovered an occupation for his time and mind and the broker's office became indispensable to him.

The tape had cured him. The changes in process were exciting, and he had found a congenial sphere. Six months elapsed, and one day Captain Charteris received a letter from Sir William, asking him to forget the past and come and dine with him on Sunday. He did so, and was surprised at the alteration in his old friend's manner. A more agreeable companion he could not have wished for.

"When are you going to send the picture round?" asked Sir William.

"When you like. I've altered Nelson into Hannibal, and polished up the Alpine scenery a bit," was the reply; "though I do not know if it will suit you."

"Of course it will. Anything of yours is sure to please me."

Charteris thought wonders would never cease.

They had dined at three o'clock ; it was about six, and if the decanters were empty their hearts were full.

"I want you to be my executor," said Sir William, suddenly.

"With pleasure ; but you do not feel ill, I hope?" replied Captain Charteris.

"No, but we never know what may happen," continued the baronet. "It is as well to be prepared. I am making money, and I have thought it best to give my solicitor instructions about my will. I'm not so young as I was once."

"Surely there is no need for you to make money."

"That is a secret. I am not so well off as people think ; the bulk of my fortune was in a Calcutta bank which went wrong. However, I am in a fair way to be rich again. Since I have been in the City I have gained experience."

"I hear every one speaks well of you."

"Do they?"

"The men who know you call you a dear old man and a

jolly fellow," replied Charteris. "They say you are the life of the whole office."

"I am very miserable sometimes," sighed Sir William.

"Why?"

"Kate won't come to me; my poor, suffering, bright-eyed Katey, and I can't go to her after what has passed. But if I am right in my calculations I shall have something for her in a few days."

"How?"

"There is a scare in Russians. I sold a 'bear' of 50,000 on Friday at 90, and I doubled it yesterday."

"The will provides——?"

"For Kate," replied Sir William; "but I hope to make you my almoner long before that is opened."

Captain Charteris willingly undertook the duty imposed upon him. They spent a pleasant evening together, and on Monday morning Sir William, as usual, was at the office long before his broker arrived. He chatted pleasantly with those who came in, and when business began watched the tape.

The scare in Russians was intensified; there was a panic in the stock.

As he sat in his chair he read, "Russian 89, 88, 87."

St. Albans Smith stood by his chair.

"Have you sold much?" he asked.

"100,000," replied the old baronet, tremblingly.

"That is a heavy account."

Tick, tick!

87, $\frac{1}{2}$, 6.

There was a pause.

The fact that Sir William was speculating heavily for the fall flew from one to the other. The rest of the tapes were deserted; every one in the office crowded round the baronet.

Again the price of Russians dropped. Everybody seemed to be selling.

Tick, tick.

86, 85, 84.

Sir William could hear his heart beat.

Tick, tick.

Russian 83, 82, 81.

Another pause, longer than the preceding ones.
Tick, tick.
81, ½, ¼, 80.
Sir William gasped for breath. He had made £10,000.
"Wa-water," he said, feebly, as his hands sank by his side and his head fell back. A smile parted his lips.
"For—Ka—Kate," he muttered, as a glassy film came over his eyes.

* * * * * *

When he came to himself he was in his own home, and Kate was bending over him, while Captain Charteris was trying to look as if he was quite surprised to see her.

"My little girl's come back at last," said Sir William, gladly.

She pressed his hand, and her eyes spoke volumes.

Sir William lived many years after that, but they were never parted again; he made her husband and her come and live with him, amassed an enormous fortune on the Stock Exchange, and died at a ripe old age of an indigestion caused by a Lord Mayor's dinner, at which he had proposed the health of "Her Majesty the Queen."

TIME AND TIDE WAIT FOR NO MAN.
A TALE OF THE TAPE.

TIME AND TIDE WAIT FOR NO MAN.

A TALE OF THE TAPE.

Mr. Robert Groome was an old-fashioned country gentleman, residing at the Grange, near Leicester. He had a nice little property, which brought him in an income of a thousand a year, in spite of the depressed condition of agriculture. At fifty he was upright as a dart, full of life and vigour, and had hair as black as a raven. He rode to hounds three days a week, shot and fished in due season. Never read a newspaper, gloried in being a bachelor, liked strong ale, old port, and good living, and boasted that he had not been to London for thirty years, travelling by stage coach the last time he had visited the metropolis. After his horses and his dogs, he bestowed most of his attention on his nephew, Owen Groome, the son of his dead brother, whom he had adopted and educated, at the end of which time he was placed in the house of Messrs. Killjoy Brothers, merchants of London and Edinburgh, as a clerk. The Killjoys were Scotchmen, and very strict.

To his uncle's surprise, Owen turned up unexpectedly one morning at the Grange.

"What has brought you here?" demanded the old gentleman.

"The 10·30 express from Euston, uncle," replied Owen.

"No nonsense, sir! I mean, what is the cause of your appearance?" said Mr. Groome, sternly.

"Killjoy Brothers and I could not agree, so I discharged them."

"You mean you have lost your situation."

"That's about the size of it," answered Owen, throwing himself into a chair.

"Humph! This requires some explanation."

"They were rather too strict for me. Old Killjoy would keep us at work till the middle of the day on Sunday, and if we hummed a tune, asked us what we meant by it. 'Hush, mon,' he'd say; 'its sinfu' to be whistlin' on the Sabbath.'"

"And I suppose you expect me to keep you in idleness, sir?" exclaimed Mr. Groome.

"Oh, no! I've got plenty of money," was the careless answer.

"Plenty of money! How much?"

"I've nearly a couple of thousand pounds at my banker's."

"The deuce you have!"

Suddenly an awful thought came into the old gentleman's head.

Had he stolen it?

Was his nephew a dishonest clerk, on whose track, even then, the police might be?

"How did you get it, sir?" he inquired.

"Easily enough, uncle."

"I want to know. How did you get it?"

"Principally out of 'Trunks' and 'Mexicans.'"

"Eh? Have you been swindling Mexicans out of their trunks?" demanded Mr. Groome, angrily.

"'Russians' helped me a little, and I mustn't say anything against 'Turks,' while 'Egyptians' were always friendly."

"Russians! Turks! Egyptians! Is the boy mad?"

"For silver, 'Great Agnes' came in very handy."

"Heaven help us! The rogue has been borrowing money from a woman."

"'Brighton' was always my favourite."

"He's been cutting a dash at a watering place! Get out of my house, sir!" thundered the squire.

"My dear uncle!"

"Not a word. I won't listen to you, sir."

"I've been talking of stocks, uncle," explained Owen.

"Eh? Stocks! What?" stammered the old gentleman.

"Railways, foreign bonds, mines."

"You said trunks."

"Of course. Grand Trunk of Canada Railroad. See?"

"Russians! Egyptians!"

"Yes; Russian bonds, Egyptian Unified stock."

"And Great Agnes. Who is she, sir? Answer me that. Some fast bit of goods, I'll warrant."

"A silver mine, uncle; that is all."

"And—and Brighton. What did you go to such an expensive place for?"

"Never was there in my life. I was speaking of Brighton A securities," laughed Owen. "I've been studying the tape."

"What is that?"

"Speculating. Killjoys found it out, and dispensed with my services, so here I am. If you like to kick me out, why——"

"No, no! I'll not be such a bear."

"Thank you. I always like a 'bull' best."

After this the explanation proceeded satisfactorily, and Owen was invited to stay as long as he liked at the Grange.

While he was on this visit to his uncle, he, having nothing better to do, fell in love with the parson's daughter, Miss Ethel Mytton, to whom he proposed, being accepted subject to his uncle's approval. Ethel was a pretty, stylish young lady, and Owen was hard hit, being very much indeed in love with her. He was just at the age to be in love with every young woman he met, and well calculated to inspire affection in return. His eyes were of a soft liquid blue, and women liked to look into them. He was not regarded as a dangerous man by men, but he was by women, for he made his power over them felt whenever he entered a room where they were. Knowing that Mr. Robert Groome had once been jilted, and had a dislike for the sex in consequence, Owen was rather afraid to broach the subject to his eccentric relative, and took care to fortify himself with an extra glass of wine at dinner, he having resolved to speak about the

L

matter before the usual game of backgammon was introduced. The uncle and nephew were sitting at dessert. A pause in the conversation gave Owen the opportunity he desired, and he took the plunge, though he would rather have trembled a little longer on the brink.

"I want to ask your permission, sir," he said, respectfully, "to—to get married."

"What!" ejaculated the squire, in a tone that made the walnuts rattle.

"I have thought it advisable to settle, and if you have no objection——"

"How are you going to live? Married life doubles, aye, trebles the expenses."

"Of course we shall be dependent on your kindness," replied Owen.

"Then the lady has no money? a very unsatisfactory bargain from a commercial point of view," said Mr. Groome. "Who is the lady, may I ask?"

"A very charming person, as I have often heard you say."

"So I know her."

"Well, it is Miss Mytton. Ethel and I have known one another since we were children. and ——"

"The parson's daughter! Yes, I know her," interrupted Mr. Groome. "She's nice enough, but a desperate flirt, they say. Look how she carried on with our neighbour, Lord Scattercash! I believe she'd have had him, if he had not lost so much money at racing. His place, Beaufort Hall, is for sale. It adjoins my property, and, in fact, I am in treaty for it. I meant it for you. It's in the market for thirty thousand pounds."

"How good of you," said the young man. "I hope my matrimonial project, uncle, will not lead you to reconsider your resolve."

"I suppose, if you've made up your mind, you will get married, whether I like it or not."

"She's the sweetest girl that ever ——"

"Pish! they're all the sweetest until you get into their power. But there! you'll say I am talking like a crusty old bachelor; and perhaps I am," replied Mr. Groome.

"You were disappointed, uncle," remarked Owen.

"I was."

"How did it happen?"

"Never mind. The past is dead and buried, and I don't like the rattling of dry bones."

"I have always been curious to hear the story."

"Oh! it's simple enough," replied Mr. Groome. "It has happened before. She was the prettiest girl in Brussels, the niece of one of our leading millionnaires, and her brother was the best billiard player in England. We were engaged. One night I called. My visit was unexpected. I heard a rustling behind a screen. I threw it down, and lo! another man was there."

"What did you do?"

"I never saw her again."

"I am sorry for you," said Owen.

"Tut! tut! boy," said Mr. Groome. "I enjoyed myself for a time in every capital in Europe. I should have been miserable with a wife—"

"And children," interjected Owen.

"Oh! there you touch me," replied Mr. Groome, with a sigh. "I have wished for children—" There was a pause.

The announcement had evidently come upon him by surprise, and, as was natural, owing to his own disastrous experience in love-making, he did not like it. He reflected. He looked on the matter in different lights. Owen did not interrupt him. He allowed him time to think, and as the muscles of the old gentleman's face relaxed, he saw that he was to have his own way. This was a great consolation to him; for he sincerely loved Miss Mytton, and fancied he was loved in return. He had kissed her on the eyes, and been kissed on the lips. Her little hand had often fondled his silken moustache, and he had toyed unreproved with her long and beautiful hair.

"Well," remarked Mr. Groome at last. "I will not oppose you, my boy. Of course, if the match turns out the reverse of what you expect, don't blame me."

"My dear uncle! As if I should think of such a thing," Owen hastened to reply.

"I'll go to London with you to-morrow, and sell my shares. You know I live up to my income, and save nothing. Horses are expensive, and I flatter myself that I have the best weight carrying hunters in all Leicestershire."

"In all England, you might say."

"Perhaps. Now, I've been keeping these shares for you. They were one pound shares when I subscribed for them, and are now worth twenty pounds a share. I've fifteen hundred of them locked up in my strong box. We will take them to London and sell them. The thirty thousand they will fetch will buy Beaufort Hall, Lord Scattercash's place, and you can take your bride there. My lawyer shall draw up the deeds at once."

"What shares are they?"

"'The Peruvian Gold Mountain' is the name of them. It is an excellent security, safe as the old lady of Threadneedle Street."

"How can I ever thank you?"

"By saying nothing more about it," replied Mr. Groome. "You are my brother's son, and I will do what I can to make you happy, though I frankly tell you I am sorry you are going to get married. I was afraid those afternoon teas and lawn tennis parties would lead to something."

"She's the sweetest——"

"Yes. You've said that before. Mind she does not turn sour."

"London will seem strange to you," observed Owen, anxious to change the conversation.

"Very. I haven't been away from this house, except to sit at quarter sessions, for thirty years. Never been in a railway train. That's something to say I liked the stage coaches. Always used to stay at the Old Bell, in Holborn —we'll go there now."

"One hour here to Rugby, two from there to London You couldn't coach it like that, uncle."

"We did not want to. The world wasn't in such a hurry in those days."

"I hope you'll like it."

"I'm sure I shan't; but no matter. I'm going for your sake. Humph! The parson's daughter. Eh! She's pretty. I think I rather admire your choice, Owen."

"I assure you, uncle, she's the sweetest——"

"There, there! don't rhapsodise. I suppose I thought so once, but I loved the wrong woman, as I told you. At any rate, she married the other fellow, and I had the satisfaction of knowing that he spent her money. Well, fill my glass; here's to the health of the future Mrs. Owen Groome, and good luck to you, my boy!"

"Thank you a thousand times, uncle," said Owen, as he helped the old squire to some comet port.

Ordering his servant to bring him writing materials, the squire wrote to his solicitor at Leicester, instructing him to conclude the purchase of the Scattercash estate without delay. It was not worth the money that was asked for it, as the tenants could not pay the high rent which had prevailed in the past, but that did not matter to the squire; it adjoined his property—he had ridden over every inch of it. There were good fox coverts on it, and it was well preserved. He should have Owen near him, which was another advantage, as he was much attached to his nephew. By the time he had won three games at backgammon he was in an excellent temper, and quite reconciled to the match; in fact, he began to think that it would be very pleasant for him to visit when he liked at the Hall, and he went to bed in a capital humour.

The jade, Fortune, however, was going to play him false. For a long time he had enjoyed uninterrupted prosperity, now the wheel was about to take a turn. She had a fine surprise in store for him. While he was rusting in the country, the world had been moving. It was all very well for him to ignore the daily papers; but they could have told him what was of interest to him. Not until he got to London did he know what had happened. The journey to Euston astonished him by the celerity with which it was accomplished. It seemed as if he had no sooner started than he arrived at his destination—trees, telegraph poles, and houses passed by him in kaleidoscopic array, and with alarming rapidity. It took his breath away, so that he hardly remarked a flirtation that his nephew was carrying on with some young ladies at the other end of the carriage. Such travelling had never occurred to his simple imagination, and a hansom cab completed his surprise. The Old

Bell was very much the same as he had known it when he was young—the gateway, the stables, and the coffee-room were the same, and over a chop he began to feel at home.

"Wonderful!" he observed. "Everything seems changed. It isn't the city I used to know—Middle-row's gone; Gray's Inn-lane's half pulled down; and they tell me the Holborn Valley's bridged over—very wonderful!—but we've no time to talk. I'll to the broker's and do my business. You can give me an introduction to your stockbroker. Send for a cab; business first, pleasure afterwards, is my motto."

Carrying a box containing his fifteen hundred shares in the Peruvian Gold Mountain, the squire got into a cab, and was driven to the broker's office, where he arrived with his nephew about two o'clock. The general waiting-room was crowded with gentlemen, who were discussing the events of the day, as far as it had progressed. There was nothing very exciting in the state of the market. Home railways were quiet; the Bank had not made an expected alteration in its rate; consequently, discounts were unaltered. Having given his card to a clerk, Mr. Groome sat down close to one of the tapes, regarding it with a special interest. He had never seen one before; indeed, he had never heard of one, and had no conception of its use or purpose. The machine was silent when he first noticed it. Presently he heard it click, click, and beheld the tape come out with something printed on it.

Owen shook hands with a couple of his friends, named Marks and Cumming. The broker was out, and Mr. Groome had to await his return.

"Glad to see you back again in town," remarked Cumming.

"Where have you been hiding yourself?" asked Marks.

"Rusticating," replied Owen. "Is there anything new?"

"Not since the death of the late lamented Queen Anne," answered Marks.

"The Dutch have taken Holland, I believe," said Cumming.

"The massacre of Gordon is more recent," returned Marks, "although you may call that ancient history now."

"He wouldn't come away," replied Cumming.

"The Government ——" began Marks.

"Oh! hang it, don't go into politics," interrupted Cumming.

"I mean, is there any movement in the markets?" continued Owen.

"Are you going to open stock?"

"Yes, if I see a good thing."

"Don't touch South Easterns," replied Cumming. "They're up four and a half."

"Follow them," exclaimed Marks.

"What! at $90\frac{1}{4}$?" said Owen, looking at the tape in the basket. "They're too high."

"If you want a 'bear,' try Peruvian," suggested Cumming.

"Anything wrong there?"

"I think it is going to everlasting smash."

Mr. Groome was alarmed at hearing Peruvian Stock spoken of in this way, but his faith in Peru was not shaken.

He had never seen a tape before, but now he watched it closely.

Tick! tick!

It sounded strange to his unaccustomed ear.

Tick! tick!

He looked up at his nephew.

"What the deuce is that, Owen, my boy?" he asked.

To Owen the tape and its uses were well known, and he hastened to enlighten his uncle on the subject.

"It's a machine," he replied, "which telegraphs all the news from a certain head-quarters, and prints it, as you see, on the tape, for the benefit of subscribers."

"By George!" said Mr. Groome, "that beats the Arabian Nights' Entertainments. Is it possible?"

He took the tape in his hand, as it kept on falling to the ground, the apparatus continuing to click in a most industrious manner.

A quantity of important news had evidently arrived, and was being transmitted by its agency to interested subscribers, who in various parts were watching its movements.

"Consols for money," he read, as the tape passed through his hand; "98, $\frac{1}{2}$, $\frac{5}{8}$, do. for account $\frac{7}{16}$ to $\frac{9}{16}$."

Mr. Groome began to like speculating, and he bought Peruvian Stock. He was every day at the office, and being a genial fellow, everyone took a liking to him.

His shares went up, and Owen advised him to sell, but he would not take his profits; though the stock was up 2 per cent. he held on for a higher price. In his anxiety for gain, he forgot that tapes wait for no man, and he let the opportunity slip.

Yes, he liked speculating. We all speculate; it is only a question of degree. If a man buys a horse or a house—a woman a dress or a carriage—it is all a speculation. Where shall we draw the line?

So a few weeks passed, and Mr. Groome could not be induced to sell. In vain Owen urged him to do so.

"Hold on; we'll get more," said the old squire.

One day he came to the office as usual, and took up the tape. What was this?

A heavy fall in Perus!

"Ah!" he cried, "Owen, come here! It's all Greek to me," he exclaimed. "But it's very extraordinary, 'pon my soul, very."

He looked up at Owen, his face being ghastly white.

"There has been trouble between the two countries for some time," replied Owen.

"Nonsense! You are doing something to the machine, just to have some fun with me."

"No, indeed, uncle."

"There has been a great battle, sir, between the Chilians and Peruvians," said Cumming.

"God bless me!"

"The Peruvians are reported as defeated."

"I never heard of it," gasped Mr. Groome.

"It is cabled that the Chilians have occupied Lima."

"I didn't know they were at war."

"It is a melancholy fact, however," replied Cumming.

"I must have been dreaming. I've been asleep, like Rip Van Winkle," exclaimed Mr. Groome.

The tape had been quiet for a moment, but its remorseless tick, tick, began again. Having it in his hand, th old gentleman could not help continuing his reading:—

"Peruvian Six per Cents., 1870, 11 to ¼; do. Five per Cents., 1872, 8 to ¼."

There was a pause, and then came the announcement, "Gold Mountain, 5-6."

This was a drop of 15 per cent., which took away a great deal from the price of his favourite bonds, which he had regarded as so very safe. To a certain extent it beggared him. All his cherished schemes with regard to his nephew and the purchase of Lord Scattercash's estate were blown to the winds. With such a loss on his stock he could not possibly purchase Beaufort Hall. He looked wildly at Owen, staring as if he had seen a spirit.

"Is this thing telling the truth?" he demanded, in a sepulchral voice.

"Yes, uncle," answered Owen.

"On your honour? Don't deceive me. I'll never forgive you if you do."

"Why, certainly."

"Then I am comparatively a ruined man."

He covered his face with his hands, and his hat fell on the floor; a dizziness came over him. He would have fallen if Owen had not solicitously put his arm round him to sustain him. Seeing his condition, Mr. Cumming brought him a glass of water, while Mr. Marks assisted Owen to support him.

"What is it?" he asked Marks. "Peruvian bonds?"

"'Gold Mountains'," replied Owen, nervously.

"Poor fellow!" said Marks, sympathisingly; "they're gone. I'm sorry for him; but I have just come from the city. There is a panic in the stock; jobbers won't make a price. That quotation on the tape is merely nominal."

"Indeed!"

"When the war is over it may recover, but at present"—He paused abruptly, and shook his head.

In a short time Mr. Groome came to himself. Owen picked up his hat and restored it to him, but was astounded to remark the alteration that had taken place in him in a short time. His hair had turned white.

Leaning on his nephew's arm, he quitted the office, and returned to the hotel, recovering from his depression as he went along.

Mr. Groome felt as if he could not go home again directly.

He had got used to the broker's office, and as he sat in the coffee room of the hotel he felt as if he would give £20 to hear the click of the tape.

It made a kind of music in his ears that he had got to like.

Shall we blame him?

There was a clever mathematician, well known in the world of science, who had liver and bacon and a pot of ale from the public-house every day for dinner all the year round, and if the supply of liver failed, or the beer turned sour, all his abstruse calculations were upset.

An old woman living in London used to watch for the gas lamp outside her window to be lit, and if the lamplighter was late, she got impatient, and used to let the whole family know it.

Was he wrong because he was longing to hear the click of the tape?

Don't you, when you are travelling, want to catch a steamer or train? Don't you want to hear the news, and look for your paper? Don't you look up and down your square or your crescent when you want your carriage?

So he stopped in London awhile, fuming and fretting and looking at the tape, but Gold Mountains did not go up again.

He had lost his chance.

"What is the matter with my hair?" he asked of his nephew on the way to the hotel, as he saw his reflection in a shop window.

"It is quite white, uncle. You will be as much astonished as I was, when you see yourself in the glass."

"Is it possible that looking at that confounded tape could have done such a thing? I—I can't quite believe it," replied the squire.

When he got a chance of seeing a glass, he looked at himself, and found that what Owen had stated was perfectly true, without an iota of exaggeration.

"By Jove! grey as a badger!" he ejaculated, as he contemplated himself in the glass. "Well, it serves me right for coming to London. What's the use of electric printing to me? What do I want with tapes? Grey, sir! Grey at fifty! Grey, by gad!"

That night they went to the theatre, and before he retired the old gentleman indulged in some brandy and water in the coffee room, and discoursed about the London of his youth, having three commercial travellers for his audience, who were in rather a disconsolate mood, as, owing to the depression in trade, they had not seen their samples for a week. He spoke of Evans'—its suppers, glees, and madrigals; of the Cider Cellars, and its quaint mock trial by jury; of the Colosseum in the Regent's Park; the Polytechnic; the Panopticon, now the Alhambra; and other sights of the past. By the time he had finished, one of his auditors was asleep. The other two had gone to bed, and, with a yawn, he followed their example, Owen carrying his candle. Before he closed his eyes that night Owen wrote Ethel a long letter, telling her what had happened.

This epistle he dispatched by the first post in the morning. Some races near London were advertised to be held on that day, and Mr. Groome took his nephew there. He lost his watch and purse, and arrived at his hotel in a very unamiable state of mind, being more than ever certain that the London of to-day was not the London of his youth, and that the English people were degenerating. In disgust he shook the dust off his feet, and went back by the express to Leicester. When in the railway carriage the noise of the wheels resembled to his fancy the click of the tape.

In imagination he was again in the broker's office. First, stocks were going up, and he was joyful; then they went down, and he was in despair. Gold Mountain was up 2; he shut his eyes. It was up 4. There it was on the tape, in black on white.

Why didn't he take his profits?

Too late!

The brave Chilians—those English of South America, the noble, warlike Chilians—had beaten the poor Peruvians, and —from pathos to bathos—prices were down. It had worn him to a shred, and he had turned grey; but there was plenty of vitality in the old man yet.

When they arrived at the Grange, Owen's first task was to call at the Rectory, and inquire after Miss Mytton, when he received the alarming intelligence that she had left home that morning, and had gone away to London. This news nearly drove him frantic—the frailty of woman astonished him. Ethel's vows had only been written in sand; poor, she cared not for him. Thunderstricken, he at once sought his uncle.

Mr. Groome had also received bad news. His solicitor wrote to inform him that Lord Scattercash had paid him a visit, to say that if Mr. Groome was not willing to complete the purchase of the property he should sue him for specific performance of contract.

"What's the matter with you?" demanded the squire.

"I shall never get over it," answered Owen.

"Over what, sir?"

'Ethel has gone away."

"She has, eh?" cried the squire. "Well, by the Lord Harry, I'm puzzled to tell which are the most uncertain—stocks or women!"

And, with a muttered anathema hurled at the whole sex, and a kind of "I told you so" air about him, he whistled to his dog, shouldered his gun, and strode out of the house, leaving Owen to console himself as best he could.

In the course of the day Owen received a letter from Ethel.

It was very brief.

"I shall always love you," she wrote. "But I cannot marry a poor man. I have left home to win a name and fortune for myself. I am going on the stage, yet, believe me, that my intercourse with you will ever seem the most pleasant period of my life."

PROMOTING A COMPANY,

OR

SHRIMPS FOR THE MILLION.

PROMOTING A COMPANY,

OR

SHRIMPS FOR THE MILLION.

In this story, for obvious reasons, neither the real names of the parties interested nor that of the company are correctly given, the object being to show up a type of men who haunt the precincts of the city, and make it their business to deceive the unwary. Not so long ago, every year proved that a large section of the public was easily gulled, and that one of the simplest ways of making money was to promote a company. Visions of large profits were the spider's web, into which the flies fell, and so long as people were not satisfied with a fair return for their money, they were dazzled by undertakings which were never destined to be honoured by the Stock Exchange with either an authorised quotation or a settling day. We may premise, however, that the main incidents in the following burlesque of a sham company are strictly founded on fact, the chief victim being still alive, though shattered in mind and body.

Our space will not allow us to refer to the giants who settled large fortunes on their wives out of the proceeds of their bubble companies, and still prosper and flourish. We shall have something to say on this point, perhaps, in a subsequent volume.

Mr. John Jeffries was a promoter of companies, and a member of some West End clubs, where baccarat is played for high stakes. Sometimes he took a run over to Monaco and punted at the tables. "Make your game, gentlemen," was a phrase he was well acquainted with. *Le jeu est fait, rien ne va plus.* He would watch the colours carefully, seize what he thought a favourable opportunity and put down his stake, and generally win. Taking his winnings, he would refrain from a laudable desire to break the bank, and next day Monaco would know him no more. He might be playing cards at the English club at Cannes, or strolling on the *Promenade des Anglais* at Nice. In fact he was a snapper-up of unconsidered trifles—all was fish that came to his net.

When he played cards he did not scruple to cheat, but he was so skilled that he seldom got found out. At poker he was a proficient, and he rarely failed to have three of a kind to beat two pair when it came to calling; he could bluff with a grave face, and was not afraid to raise the ante on a couple of trays. When he was once paying a flying visit to Ostend, he was very neatly bowled out. The game was unlimited loo, and he was playing at the club. A looker-on whispered to him, "I will stand in with you."

Jeffries shook his head.

"I say I will stand in with you, sir," repeated the stranger.

"No."

"I say I will!"

"Why should you?" asked Jeffries, in the same low tone.

"You are playing crooked, and I can prove it."

"All right. Keep quiet," said Jeffries, inwardly inclined to bite the fellow's head off.

"I said I should stand in," remarked the 'cute stranger with a smile; and during the rest of the play he kept account of Jeffries' gains.

When the latter rose from the table, they went outside and divided the spoil according to arrangement.

"Are you satisfied?" asked Jeffries, savagely, as the man pocketed the notes and gold.

"Quite; thank you. Ah! you're a wonder," was the reply.

"What?"

"A masterpiece. How did you do it. Captain Threestars was playing crooked too.

"Was he?"

"Yes. He had a card up his sleeve.

"Why didn't you stand in with him?"

"I spotted you first."

"Just like my luck."

"But how you could play against Captain Threestars puzzles me."

"My dear fellow," replied Jeffries, carelessly; "if he had a card up his sleeve, I always have two in my boots."

Yet at the age of forty he was no better off than he had been at twenty-five. All he possessed was a few hundreds in his drawing account at the City and Country Bank, the manager of which had such an opinion of his character and integrity, that he would neither discount for him or allow him to overdraw. In fact, he knew him too well to allow him such favour, but at the same time he did one thing for him, which managers of banks ought not to be permitted to do, by law. It often happened that Jeffries used to run his account so low, that without actually closing it, he would not have a balance of more than £5 to his credit. Nevertheless, he would give cheques with characteristic recklessness, and instead of returning them marked "N. S." or "not sufficient," the manager would return them endorsed "Refer to Drawer," which saved him from unpleasant consequences.

Many stories were told of him in the City.

At Monte Carlo he was hard up, and it was necessary to pay expenses. His hotel bill had been running on for three weeks. He lived like a prince, did Jeffries, denying himself nothing. Going to the *rouge et noir* table, he watched and waited, cat-like; he saw that red turned up thirty times in succession; he pounced, putting all he had on black; the colour won. He left his stake, and black was successful five times running. He took up his money, went away, paid his bill, and put the rest in a drawer in his bedroom. An hour afterwards he went to look at it. The drawer had been tampered with, but the cash was still there; he put it in his pocket, and went back to the tables; the result was he played again and lost all he had.

At the Magatherium Club he was giving young Lord Headlong a dinner for a purpose. He never threw a dinner away. *Écarté* was proposed; they adjourned to the card-room and played. His lordship lost £1,000.

"Hang it," he cried, "you always win."

"So much the better for me," replied Jeffries, folding up his lordship's cheque.

"I can't get in at all."

"So much the worse for you."

"Give me a chance."

"Certainly, if it gives me an equal one."

Jeffries did not care to give an opponent any advantage; he could not waste time in frivolity. Time with him was money, and he held that poverty was worse than a sin—it was a crime.

"We had a ripe Stilton at dinner," continued Lord Headlong. "Come to the dining-room, we will each have a plate, and put a maggot in the middle."

"Well?"

"The first maggot off wins."

"What is the stake?"

"Double or quits."

"Agreed," said Jeffries.

Entering the dining-room, Jeffries called a waiter.

"The Stilton," he exclaimed. "Two plates."

"Yes, sir."

And lowering his voice to a whisper, so as not to be heard by Lord Headlong, he added, "Hot mine."

The waiter nodded, and carried out his orders.

Lord Headlong selected a fine fat maggot; so did Jeffries. They held them in the bowls of two spoons, and dropped them on the plates as near the centre as possible. His lordship's made tracks for the side; Jeffries' jumped right off in two jumps.

"D—— the brute," said Lord Headlong in disgust. "I never saw such a beastly lively maggot."

And with an ill grace he paid the second thousand.

But the most extraordinary thing of all was Jeffries lived for three years on a brickbat.

This was how he did it.

He invented what he called an aërated brick, for which he took out a patent. He had a sample brick made of white clay. It was perforated with holes, from which it was supposed to derive its hygienic and sanitary properties. He influenced men of position in it, and got up companies to bring it out, which collapsed one after the other, but he secured the promotion money. One day he met the well-known Mr. X. coming out of his private room. Mr. X. had often seen him hanging about the office, but, taking him for one of the Touting Brigade, had always refused to see him. He had under his arm a neat brown paper parcel, tied with pink tape.

"Can I speak with you privately?" asked Jeffries.

"What for?" asked X.

"To propose a plan. There is a fortune in this little parcel."

Mr. X. led him inside.

"What does it contain?" he asked, "a steam-engine?"

"No. I have driven my carriage on it, but I haven't pushed it lately."

"Is it a new motive-power?"

"Again, no! I have lived on it for three years, and I want to interest an enterprising gentleman like yourself in it. Let me show it you."

He undid wrapper after wrapper and disclosed a brick.

"Aid me in getting up a company for it," he added.

"Where are your works?"

"We want none. The public will subscribe. They like bricks."

But he had come to the wrong shop this time. Mr. X. gently pushed him out of the door, and threw his brick after him.

In addition to this, we may mention that he had a small house at Bexley Heath, where he resided with his wife and six children. A peculiar thing about rogues is that they generally have a wife and family to drag down when they fall. Sometimes the family ties are useful, they excite sympathy among his acquaintances: "for the sake of his wife and little ones, you know," is quite a familiar phrase. We have all heard it, and overlooked misdeeds. During his varied and chequered career, Jeffries had been the proprietor of a sauce, also a hair raiser. There was no hidden sarcasm in this, though he was saucy enough and had often raised people's hair by his wild-cat schemes. It sold well, and he disposed of the patent for a considerable sum, when at his lowest ebb he had started a barber's shop, where you could have your hair cut and get a bowl of soup for fourpence. His inventive genius did not stop here. Feeling that the bronchial sufferings of humanity ought to be relieved, he made up a cough mixture, which he advertised very extensively. Thousands had reason to bless it, though the principal ingredients were tincture of opium and syrup of squills. He sold this too, and started the Sea Water Supply Company, the bill for which however, he could not get through Parliament. He followed this with the Marriage Mart and Universal Matrimonial Agency, which came to an end through the conduct of the infuriated persons whom he introduced to one another. They contracted marriage; they did not like it, so they came down in a body, and wrecked his premises. Jeffries narrowly escaped with his life, one metamorphosed spinster of doubtful age threatening him with death.

He next interested himself in an Ærial Electric Locomotion Company, but though the company eventually went up in the air, the machines never did. His genius after that blossomed forth in the West-End Sedan Chair Company, it being his idea that fashionable ladies would like to be conveyed to parties and balls in Sedan chairs, as they were in the days of good Queen Anne. His models were highly approved, and the uniforms of his bearers pronounced perfect. Some old East Indians, who had not forgotten their palanquin journeys, took shares, but the public persistently preferred cabs and broughams, so the West-End Sedan Chair Company collapsed; but he had made a few thousands out of it. From all his undertakings, rotten and bad as they undoubtedly were, he cleared money, and might have done well if his evil genius had not at last induced him to go in for electric lights. Even then he would have made 120 per cent., but like a good many more victims, he held on for 300. It galvanised him. It shook him up; and he facetiously called the company The Electric Liver and

Lights. Gas was to be nowhere. Pimlico, Fulham, and the districts where the hideous gasometers find a home were jubilant, for the inhabitants thought they would be done away with, but the gasometers still exist, and the Electric Liver and Lights is dead.

Though Jeffries was a schemer, we may mention that he was passionately attached to his wife and children, who were all very good-looking; the boys being handsome and manly, the girls beautiful. If he schemed it was for the sake of his family. Call him a mercenary villain, if you will; it was not for himself he laboured. He stood at nothing where money was concerned. His wife and he had known one another in their youth. He loved her; but they were parted. They met again, and were married. He worked hard, and never took a holiday. If he went abroad it was to make money. If he was harsh to men he was a child to a woman. His wife sings an old song, he turns away his head and cries; yet he would crush a man under his heel in business. On a Sunday he had taken his family to Windsor to see the beeches and the deer, and romped about like a boy in the old park. On Monday he was issuing prospectuses of an undertaking which would ruin hundreds.

He had once been bold enough to stand for Parliament. It was a metropolitan constituency for which he stood, but he retired in disgust before going to the poll. Innumerable deputations of women waited upon him, representing every real and fancied grievance: one lot objected to pictures representing nude studies being exhibited in the galleries; another wanted to regulate the social evil, representing that shop girls should be watched by the police, as comparatively respectable women had taken the place of the professional abandoned creatures of twenty years ago; in fact, he had no idea of the number of busybodies there are ready to ventilate grievances, evils, and abuses, until he endeavoured to become a public man.

His great friend who assisted him in all his enterprises was a man of about his own age, named Charles Bayldon, who had been a bookmaker, but was obliged to relinquish that lucrative profession because he one Monday neglected to settle with his creditors, and was posted at Tattersall's Subscription Room as a defaulter. He now described himself as an agent, and did a little business for customers, whom he met principally in taverns, though he was privileged to transact business in one of the two rooms which Jeffries rented in Bucklersbury. One morning in early spring Jeffries arrived at the Cannon Street Station at ten o'clock, and proceeded to his office, where he found Bayldon waiting for him, he having been summoned by letter to attend to new and important business. They shook hands, lighted their cigars, told the half-a-crown-a-week boy, who acted in the capacity of clerk, that they were visible to nobody, and retired into the inner room, which was marked "private."

"What's in the wind now?" asked Bayldon, expectantly.

"Money, my dear fellow," replied Jeffries, who was always optimistic in his views. "Money, and lots of it, I hope."

"Another company?"

"Just so," said Jeffries, oracularly

"I should have thought you had had enough of that line of business," remarked Bayldon, "after the Marriage Mart, the Sedan, the Ærated Brick, and the Electric Liver and Lights."

"This time I shall make a hit," interrupted Jeffries, "a palpable hit. The idea occurred to me all in a moment. I had been spending a few days at Southend, and walked over to Leigh. Now, what is Leigh famous for?"

"Mud," replied Bayldon, stroking his moustache with a ruminant air.

"No, my good man, it is where all the shrimps come from. I made the acquaintance of a fisherman named Trawler. He has got half a dozen smacks and nets to sell, with an old barn thrown in. We can buy the lot for a song, and have a going concern, lock, stock, and barrel."

"What for?"

"The London and Provincial Shrimp Breeding, Catching and Canning Company, Limited; works at Leigh, Essex," said Jeffries, earnestly. "You see, land for breeding purposes could easily be acquired. We shall soon have money in the bank."

"The mud bank, you mean."

"You know what I mean. We will buy a part of the foreshore of the river. Now, pay attention. Shrimps are scarce, shrimps are dear, and they are undoubtedly a favourite article of food with the masses. I ask you, what a Bank Holiday would be without shrimps? Would not Hampstead Heath become a howling waste, and Greenwich a desert without its teas and shrimps at ninepence a head? You can get your Souchong mildly tempered with Pekoe at two shillings per pound, but you cannot obtain the indispensable, the appetising, the all-absorbing shrimp for less than sixpence a quart, and the supply is deficient at that. The L. and P S. B. C. and C. Company will cheapen and tend to still more popularise the shrimp. It will be a food for the people. The eye of the dyspeptic will glisten, for your fine fat fresh shrimp is as easy of digestion as an oyster; the innocent face of childhood will be wreathed with smiles, for what child ever despised his shrimp? the facial muscles of the horny handed son of toil will relax; the Blue Ribbon man will feel his heart expand, and the drinker will become gay, for all know what the shrimp is to a thirsty man; the comely matron will become more comely; in fact, we shall supply a long felt want. It will be a sweet boon to one and all, to rich and poor—the coroneted earl and the ill-fed, underpaid artisan. What the people want is cheap shrimps and plenty of them.

John Jeffries paused to get his breath.

"What do you think of it?" he asked, presently.

"Very good," replied Bayldon. "The possibilities of the company are infinite. We could add dabs, and might rise to oysters."

"Of course. I never thought of dabs or natives."

"And yet you are a dab at astonishing the natives," said Bayldon, perpetrating a mild joke.

"Don't be frivolous. Sit down and draw up the usual document. 'Articles of Agreement entered into between Charles Bayldon of the one part, acting on behalf of the London and Provincial Shrimp Breeding, Catching, and Canning Company, Limited, hereinafter called the Company, and Mr. Timothy Trawler, for the purchase of ——' You know how to go on."

"Yes, yes. I've got it by heart."

"Then write out the prospectus. I want to get the advertisements out as quick as possible. Offices of the company, here ; bankers, City and Country. Put old File down as solicitor. My father-in-law and your brother will do as directors, with the baronet as chairman."

Taking pen, ink, and paper, Bayldon began to write facilely, for this kind of work was familiar to him, and while he is at work we will say a word about the directors. Mr. Morley Morley. the father-in-law of Jeffries, was a tenant farmer, of no means, of the Uplands Farm, near Chelmsford, which sounded well in the prospectus. Mr. Christopher Tatton Bayldon kept a grocer's shop at Highgate Rise, and had confined himself to his Christian names for some time past, owing to an irregularity in his accounts discovered by his creditors under his third bankruptcy, which had necessitated his withdrawal from public life for the space of six months on a judge's order. The baronet alluded to was Sir Augustus de Sarcenet Drake, who, for a couple of pounds a week, payable in advance, was always ready and willing to allow Jeffries to use his name in connection with his undertakings. He lodged in a small road, built on an estate called Bolingbroke Park, in a southern suburb, but he was invariably described as Sir Augustus de S. Drake, Bolingbroke Park, S.W., which looked very well in print.

"I've done the prospectus," said Bayldon, laying down his pen after a time.

"Very well ; let us see how you've baited the hook," replied Jeffries, who had been busily figuring in a note book as to the estimated profits of the first twelve months, the amount of income over expenditure showing several thousand pounds net, and an approximate dividend of 50 per cent.

He looked as pleased as the young broker who went into the "House," and by a fluke made a sovereign in a minute, and spent the rest of the day calculating, if he made a pound a minute every day, how much he would be worth at the end of the year.

Bayldon handed him a sheet of foolscap paper, on which was written—

"The London and Provincial Shrimp Breeding, Catching,

and Canning Company Limited." Capital, £30,000 in 30,000 shares of £1 each. Payable 5s. per share on application, and 15s. on allotment.

"Incorporated under the Companies' Acts 1862 to 1880, whereby the liability of shareholders is strictly limited to the amount of their shares.

DIRECTORS.

Sir Augustus de S. Drake, Bart., Bolingbroke Park, S.W.
Morley Morley, Esquire, The Uplands, Chelmsford, Essex.
Christopher Tatton, Esquire, The Rise, Highgate, London.
With power to add to their number.

Bankers: The City and Country, Bartholomew Lane, E.C.

Solicitor: W Sharpe File, Clement's Inn.

Secretary pro tem.: Charles Bayldon, Esquire.

Office: 175, Bucklersbury, London.

"That won't do," said Jeffries.

"What do you object to?" asked Bayldon.

"You ought to know better than to put yourself down as secretary."

"I forgot."

"Of course you did. Hang it all! we must start the company at the expense of the secretary."

"I only put myself in temporarily; we will advertise for a victim at once."

"Yes. We want one with about £2,000," said Jeffries.

Bayldon was a practical man, and saw the point at once. He was always sharp, short, and business-like. They said in the City that he was the hero of the longest and shortest correspondence on record.

His tailor had written to him every three months for seven years for his account. At last he replied:—"Sir,—Your letters to hand. If you annoy me any more I shall put the matter in the hands of my solicitor."

He met a lady at a party. She had some money, and he thought he would like to make her Mrs. Bayldon. To take a cab to her home would have cost time and cash, so he wrote:—

"Dear Madam,
    "Do you want to marry?
            "Yours truly,
                "C. BAYLDON."

To which the lady replied:

"Dear Sir,
    "Certainly.
            "Yours truly,
                "R. SMITH."

He wrote again:

"Dear Madam,
    "Will you marry me?
            "Yours truly,
                "C. BAYLDON."

The reply came:

"Dear Sir,
    "Certainly not.
            "Yours truly,
                "R. SMITH."

So Bayldon remained a bachelor.'

"The baronet is a good card," remarked Bayldon.

"I count on Sir Augustus to float the company, and the public to support it," answered Jeffries.

"He wants his fees in advance."

"Oh! I always humour Sir Augustus, though I once lost a good director by giving him his money before it was due: he withdrew; it frightened him; he thought the concern looked fishy."

"That's what they'll say of the Shrimp Breeding, Catching, and Canning Company."

"I spoiled a respectable man," sighed Jeffries, thinking of his lost director.

"Good L——! it wouldn't spoil me," laughed Bayldon.

"We can sell for cash and go on credit," continued Jeffries, recurring to his shrimps.

"You can acquire a retail business for a small sum. There is old Loader, who keeps a fish stall near the station, his stock usually consists of two lobsters and a pint of shrimps."

Jeffries laughed.

"It is a very old established business," added Bayldon, "and will go cheap to an immediate purchaser for prompt cash."

There was another laugh.

"By G—! old man, you're in it," Bayldon concluded, "and it will be good news for the baronet."

"Yes, he'll see a chance of paying his washerwoman," remarked Jeffries, "and his eyes will glisten."

"I've heard him say she's a tight 'un."

"I reckon she is about the only creditor he does pay."

"Laundresses and bakers are troublesome, and so are milkmen," exclaimed Bayldon, reflectively.

"Do you speak from experience?"

"Yes, I often drink champagne at home, though I greatly prefer milk."

"Why?"

"Because I can't get milk without money, and I've always plenty of champagne in the house; the wine merchant only sends in his bill once in six or twelve months."

"Well, how do you like my scheme?" asked Jeffries.

"It will be the greatest success you ever invented," returned Bayldon.

"I thought of bringing out a lead mine, but—"

"Bah! mines are no good; mines stink. Now listen to the prospectus."

"I am ready."

Bayldon began to read the particulars he had jotted down.

This was rather a lengthy affair, so we will only take the heads of it. The directors invited subscriptions for the shares of the above-named company, to enable them to purchase the fishing smacks, nets, premises, and plant generally of Timothy Trawler, Esq., fish merchant, of Leigh

Essex, and to extend and develop the already existing large business done in catching and forwarding shrimps to the London and other markets; also to breed, pot, and can shrimps, a very lucrative trade in which could be done by a judicious outlay of capital. All companies engaged in the fishing trade were making enormous profits, and the company would have almost an exclusive field, which justifies the directors in anticipating a most satisfactory return to the shareholders.

"The only contract entered into is one dated the 10th day of May between Mr. Timothy Trawler of the one part, and Charles Bayldon of the other part, as trustee of the company, for the purchase of certain property, which, together with the articles of association, can be seen at the office of the solicitor.

"Prospectuses and forms of application may be obtained from the bankers, solicitor, or from the secretary at the company's offices. In the event of no allotment being made to an applicant, the deposit will be returned in full. If a smaller number of shares are allotted than applied for, the surplus deposit will be credited towards the amount payable upon allotment."

Then followed a dissertation on shrimps, their market value, their fecundity, and their popularity. It was argued that a plentiful supply at sixpence the quart, retail measure, would enormously increase the consumption, and one came to the end of the prospectus with the firm conviction impressed on the mind that the social elevation of the masses was only to be effected by the means of cheap and abundant shrimps, for which the people of England had long been craving. They were to regenerate mankind, and build up the condition of succeeding generations of this great empire. One marvelled why the apostle of shrimp culture had never risen in our midst before, but the gap was to be stopped at last, and the country saved from speedy perdition. The adipose tissue and manly bearing of our shrimp-fed population in Essex was pointed to with pride, and it was clear that halcyon days were in store for us.

Jeffries made a few corrections, excisions, and additions, after which he expressed himself satisfied with the prospectus. The same day he went to Leigh with Bayldon, and bought the property that old Trawler wished to sell. In fact the boats were worn out, the nets full of holes, the boilers leaky, and the barn in a tumble-down condition. Trawler had had enough of shrimping, and wanted to go into the beer-house line, which offered a more congenial sphere to him. He was glad enough to get rid of his plant at any price, but Jeffries was equally pleased to obtain it, because it gave him something to work upon. Returning to London, he gave the manifold copy of the prospectus to the papers and awaited results. The baronet seeing his name in the paper, over his matutinal coffee, was one of the first to call. Having an income, as he would often observe jocosely, of nothing a year, paid quarterly, he recognised the fact that he was entitled to something, and did not deem it prudent to let capital, however small, lie idle. Money was at all times needed by him, for he had an unquenchable thirst, which was as expensive to him as a taste for orchids is to a duchess. Fully expecting him, Jeffries had a cheque ready on his desk, which, after shaking hands, he presented. It was for a month's pay as director at two guineas a week, and Sir Augustus pocketed it with a nod intended to convey his thanks.

"What's this new swindle?" he asked, irreverently.

"My dear sir, how can you talk like that?" replied Jeffries, greatly shocked, "it's the grandest idea of the present century."

"Humbug!" said Sir Augustus, "any one would think you were a Mahdi, going to bring about a millennium; but you can give me some shares if you think they will go to a premium."

"Sure to. We shall have them at three above par before the week's out. I'm having fifty got ready in your name."

"Can I borrow anything on them?" inquired the baronet, his eyes twinkling in a merry manner.

"Why not?"

"Say as collateral security for a bill of £170."

"Try it; they ought to be as good as a bank note to you," said Jeffries.

"Or a new pawn ticket," laughed Sir Augustus; "their

value will only decrease with age. Oh, you can do it. I believe you'd take the pence out of a blind man's hat, or run away with a railway arch if you could carry it."

"How well he knows me," remarked Jeffries.

"Got any specimens? Pegwell Bays are my favourites," asked Sir Augustus.

"You must come down to the fishery," answered Jeffries. "This time we are on the right track, and have a sure fortune in hand."

Sir Augustus de Sarcenet Drake whistled.

"Upon my word, Jeffries," he remarked, "I sometimes fancy you tell 'em till you believe what you are saying. However, it does not make a pin's worth of difference to me. All I want is a cheque in advance. When do you hold your first board meeting?"

"You shall have due notice," was the rather dry answer.

"Where's Charley?"

"Bayldon? Oh, he's round the corner, I suppose. You generally know where to find him."

The baronet waved an adieu with his ungloved and not scrupulously clean hands—they said all his landed property was under his nails—leaving Jeffries to speculate as to the success of his new venture. Jeffries looked at his window on which was painted, "Mr. John Jeffries, Financial Agent," and at a slip of paper placed underneath, on which was written the name of the new company. He could not help feeling that he was a clever fellow, but at the same time he wondered how it was he never made a fortune. It was true he lived. But how? From hand to mouth, as it were. Figuratively, the wolf was always barking at his door. He longed for rest; he wanted to get out of the busy, whirling maelstrom of City life. In reality, this man liked pastoral pursuits; he could have been contented in a cottage with a large garden, growing fruit and flowers and vegetables, rearing poultry, and varying the monotony of such a life with a little fishing and shooting, always provided that he had his wife and children with him. But these things were not to be his. Similarly to Ixion he was bound to his wheel, and if he wanted to wear purple and fine linen he must spin to get it. While he was plotting and planning his clerk brought him a lady's card, which had engraved on it "Mrs. Haydon, Brook Street, Grosvenor Square." He ordered his visitor to be admitted. She was a handsome, middle-aged woman, dressed in deep mourning. She had blue eyes and brown hair, and was of the Irish type. Mary Haydon had married an elderly man for his money. She had not loved him. In fact, she had never yet seen the man she could love. She was a pretty woman and a flirt. Now that her husband was dead she wanted association, feeling that she could not live alone. But she could not find what she wanted, but directly she saw Jeffries she felt that she could love him. It is so with many of us. We look round for years. At last we say, "This is the one I want." We know not why; we care not why. Yet it is so. Let each one ask his own heart Jeffries was not a handsome man for a woman to fall in love with, but he was fascinating, and pleased women. He saw from her facial expression that she liked him, and he determined to take advantage of the weakness and get her money. All the time, however, he was strictly true and loyal to his wife and children. In her hand she held a newspaper, in which she had marked an advertisement of his. It set forth, among other things, that he was prepared to give advice to intending investors, and she explained her business at once by informing him that she was the widow of a physician who had left her fifteen thousand pounds, invested at three per cent., half of which she wanted to speculate with. She wished to see what she could do with seven thousand. At present this sum only brought her in an income of two hundred and ten pounds. What could she do for the best? She had heard that in the City, by taking shares in companies, she could treble or quadruple it. Was this true? Did not Electric Lights show a large profit?"

"They did not," replied Mr. Jeffries, "but he had in his hands the very thing that would just suit her," and he presented her with a proof of the prospectus of the L. and P. S. B. C. and C. Company, upon the prospects of which he took advantage of the opportunity to dilate.

"I am willing," said Mrs. Haydon, "to follow your advice, but I do hope you are not mistaken in your estimate of the probable profits of this concern, as I have young children, whose future I have to study."

"My dear madam, the prospectus speaks for itself. Everyone eats shrimps. We shall do an enormous business. You have come just in time," replied Jeffries, "for I expect that by to-morrow the shares will have been applied for twice over."

"I heard of a lady who invested in some oil shares, and after a time the wells dried up."

"Shrimps can never be exhausted, and people will eat them as long as England is a country."

So eloquent and enthusiastic did Jeffries become, that Mrs. Haydon was persuaded to invest her surplus cash in the company. He called several times on her at her house. In the end she gave the promoter a cheque for seven thousand pounds he presenting her in return with a receipt for the amount, promising to have the shares ready for her in a day or two. His first care was to go to her bank and get the money in notes and gold. These he put in his side pocket. He felt as if he was treading on air. The idea of devoting the cash to the interests of the company did not occur to him for a moment. Feeling that it was a time when inspiration might be derived from the consumption of champagne, he strolled into a restaurant, where he met several friends, who congregated round him at once.

"Hullo, Jeff!" cried one.

"Here's old Jeff, in his best stride," said another. "Hurrah for Jeff!"

"He's looking more jolly than he did over Electric Liver and Lights!" remarked a third.

"What will you have?" said a fourth. "Perrier Jouet or Pommery Greno? Anything you like. What's it to be? Pommery or Moet?"

"Have you been to the 'House'—how are prices?" asked Jeffries, while the wine was being opened.

"The markets are firm. Your favourites, Chatham Prefs., are up 2. But I say, what is this new scheme of yours?"

He handed them each a prospectus.

"By Jove! that's a glorious idea! Supply a want, you know," exclaimed one of his friends.

"Shrimps are the thing; I always said so," remarked a second.

"They've been neglected too long," observed a third.

"Don't forget us when you make the allotment," said the fourth.

"No, no; Jeff never forgets his friends," replied the first speaker. "By G—! Jeff's a good fellow."

The object of this panegyric was about to raise his glass to his lips when a man in a threadbare coat and a shabby hat looked in at one of the doors.

Two years ago this man had been rich, but he was dazzled by the Aerated Patent Brick or the West-End Sedan—it does not matter which—and he lost his all. Since then he had haunted Jeffries, who always fled at the sight of him.

It was a case of the fly out of the mustard pot; he was off.

"Goodbye," he said, hurriedly, setting down his glass. "Pressing engagement—excuse me."

He rushed to a side door, and was soon out of sight.

"Villain!" yelled the ruined speculator, gnashing his teeth.

"Ha! ha!" laughed the friends; "one of Jeff's ghosts," and there was a chorus of "Ha! ha! ha!"

Jeffries walked away eastward until he got into unfrequented streets, and communed with himself. He was inclined to let the company take care of itself now that he had got Mrs. Haydon's money. That the company never could and never would pay he knew perfectly well. It's explosion was only a question of time. If he could get abroad and change his name he would be able to start in some business, and send for his wife and children. To a man like himself this was an alluring prospect. He could not resist the temptation. What did it matter to him if he betrayed his friend Bayldon, and involved the name-lending baronet in disgrace? Such men as he only live for themselves. The very nature of their business makes them selfish. He would do it. Yes, he would throw care to the winds; and instead of going back to the office he went to a railway station, and booked himself to Paris. It was nothing new for him to leave his wife for days at a time without giving her any notice. She was used to such eccentricities on his part. Bayldon, however, was alarmed when his partner did not make his appearance on the following day. He guessed that something had happened. What it was he did not know until Mrs. Haydon called again at the office in Bucklersbury, finding him there. She had done what she ought to have done before making the investment—that is, she had consulted her friends, who had advised her that she had done the wrong thing; so she wanted to sell her shares, and get her money back. But this was not so easy in practice as it looked in theory. Subscriptions did not come in very fast. The public fought shy of the company, and there was no market for the security. Then she told Bayldon how much money she had given to Jeffries, which opened his eyes.

"You will never see him again," he said, angrily, for he felt that he had been made a fool of, and left in the lurch.

"Why not? I—I do not understand you," replied Mrs. Haydon.

"He has absconded."

"Then he is a swindler."

"Call him what you like. By this time he is in Paris, if he does not go to Monte Carlo direct. That's his loadstone."

Mrs. Haydon wrung her hands tearfully.

"Oh! how cruelly I have been deceived, and my poor children robbed, but I, weak woman as I am, will follow him to the end of the world if necessary and get my money back."

Her pride was wounded and her jealousy aroused.

"If you can. It is sunk in a morass."

"You are in league with him, you are one of the gang of villains."

"I assure you, I have not had a shilling of the money," replied Bayldon, who put his hat on his head and rushed wildly from the office, not knowing what fresh trouble he would have to face if he remained there.

Mrs. Haydon did not attempt to follow him. Jeffries was the man she wanted; she determined to hunt him down, and being a woman of considerable energy she set about it at once. Requiring assistance she engaged the services of a private detective, who ascertained that a gentleman answering the description of Jeffries had gone by the night mail to Paris on the preceding evening. Following up this slight clue, they started together for the French capital, where they found distinct traces of the absconder, but the bird had flown, they knew not whither. On a forlorn hope they went on to Monte Carlo, arriving there about ten o'clock on a beautiful moonlight night.

"You will want rest, madam," suggested her companion.

"No," she replied bravely, "my brain is on fire; to the tables."

They proceeded without making any alteration in their travelling attire to the gambling saloon. Here they saw Jeffries, who rose dejectedly from his seat and muttered, "All lost! all gone! Oh, my poor wife!"

"His wife! he talks of his wife," hissed Mrs. Haydon.

Listlessly he strolled into the gardens, the sound of the music swelling on the night air; he had gambled and lost, that was evident enough. Mary Haydon pursued him, the detective was close behind. Jeffries paused under a tree, against the trunk of which he leant; his eyes were downcast, and he trembled violently, as if stricken with the ague; the rustle of a dress aroused him; he looked up, Mrs. Haydon stood before him, their eyes met.

"My money!" shrieked she, "the money you robbed me of; I demand it back."

"Go to the croupier," replied Jeffries, recklessly.

"Have you lost it?"

"Every sovereign."

"Wretch!" cried the maddened woman, "you shall pay for this with your life."

She drew a pistol from her pocket, the polished barrel flashed before his eyes, and he saw that she intended to shoot him.

"Hold!" he exclaimed, "do not stain your hands with my blood."

"You think to escape me?"

"On the contrary, I will save you the trouble of killing me."

With a sudden movement, Jeffries snatched the pistol from her hand, put it to his head, pulled the trigger, and ere the report had died away fell down dead at her feet.

The servants of the Casino, accustomed to such scenes, and ever on the alert, came with an ambulance, and took the body away quickly, before the crowd could fix their morbid gaze upon the lifeless clay.

Mary Haydon was avenged!

But at what a price!

She had not meant to go so far, for to the last she had cherished a forlorn hope that she could make the unhappy man love her.

Certainly she felt the loss of her money—women always do feel this kind of thing more than men—but she would have set this off against his love.

Sinking on her knees with an agonised cry, she clasped her hands, and exclaimed, in a voice that quivered with emotion, "Good God! What have I done?"

Then she fell forward on her face in a dead faint.

And still the music floated on the breeze, and the croupier said, mechanically, "Make your game."

THE DEFAULTER.

THE DEFAULTER.

Mr. Poppleton Cripps was a widower without children; his love for his wife was a sacred recollection, and he would not marry again; but to supply an aching void in his heart he had adopted, at an early age, the child of an old friend. She was but a little girl when she came to live with Mr. Cripps, at Belgrave House, in the pretty village of Thaydon, in Derbyshire, and all remembrance of her infancy soon faded from her mind. Nellie Vine grew up to be a very pretty young lady; called Mr. Cripps father, and reigned supreme in his household. When the old gentleman noticed the admiring glances that men bestowed upon her, he said that the time was coming when he would lose her. The thought caused him considerable pain, for he felt that life would be a blank without this winsome, bright-eyed fairy, who made sunshine for him. He was not a selfish man, and if it was for her happiness to go he would part with her; but, at the same time, he determined to find out a working man for her husband. She should not be the wife of any fortune hunter. Mr. Cripps was a lead smelter; his works were at Thaydon. He had made plenty of money, and could afford to be openhanded. Nellie was not the kind of girl to throw herself away. She had a high ideal, and the man she married would have to realise it. He must be the soul of honour. Wealth she valued no more than she did good looks. She wanted a man amongst men; a hero in the battle of life—honest, pure, godly, with a mind stocked with varied knowledge. Alas! for her maiden aspirations. What she required is very hard to find in this degenerate world of ours.

At eighteen, Nellie Vine was the idol of the villagers; she was good to them, and a true friend. It is not too much to say that she made every one with whom she came in contact feel better. Up to the time our story opens she had seen no one whom she could love, but at length the time came when she met her fate. Mr. Poppleton Cripps made the acquaintance of George Franklin, a stockbroker in the city, who acted for him in the purchase of some shares. Franklin pleased the old man, because he saw his weaknesses and flattered him. At the time they met, Franklin was in difficulties, and as Poppleton Cripps was operating largely, his business was of great advantage to him. At length the broker was invited to dinner at the country house, where he saw Miss Vine, whom he paid attention to. Love with him was an abstraction, he had been in and out of love half a dozen times; it was with him merely the means to an end. While Nellie sighed and longed for her ideal man to come, he prayed for a woman with plenty of cash. He was a handsome, fascinating fellow, and it was nothing new for women to fall desperately in love with him. He was sick and tired of being loved. He considered it dangerous for him to be civil to a woman, because she was sure to begin by liking and end by loving him. Although he hated work he worked hard, for it brought him money, and he liked to enjoy himself. His motto was, "Work, wine, and women." "You can get the third without the first," he would say, " but, by G—, you can't command the second." Mr. Cripps had been confidential with him. He knew that the old lead smelter was extremely wealthy; he saw that Nellie was a charming girl, and he resolved to render himself as agreeable as he could to Cripps, and by degrees win the girl. Good looking, well dressed, a perfect gentleman, and well informed, it was not a difficult task for him to make Nellie care for him. But he mistook her character; he thought she would be dazzled by his showy manner, and did not think that it was necessary to convice her of his sterling worth. This was the rock he split upon, as we shall see. George Franklin had been several times to Thaydon; he frequently came on Saturday and stayed until Monday; he had mortified the flesh by going to the village church with Nellie, and listening to an excruciatingly bad sermon ; but, to his surprise, he did not make the impression on her mind that he had expected. She was a better judge of character than Mr. Cripps, and she was not quite satisfied with her father's new friend. Cripps did all he could to bring them together. One evening in summer Franklin was dining at Thaydon ; the wine had been placed on the table. Nellie had retired, for Mr. Cripps liked to have a quiet hour over his wine. The broker had not been in very good form at dinner ; his troubles were increasing ; he had a large sum to pay at the end of the month. It was then the twenty-eighth ; where to get the money he did not know. A desperate idea had occurred to him. If Nellie would consent to marry him he would not attempt to settle with his creditors ; he would hide in the country, allow himself to be posted as a defaulter, and trust to Cripps to get him out of his difficulties. This was a bold scheme ; but he was worried and bothered, and scarcely knew what to do.

"Now, I want your opinion of these wines," exclaimed Mr. Poppleton Cripps, as the butler placed the decanters of port on the table.

"You shall have it," replied Franklin, helping himself to the olives. I have been working hard. To-day was 'contango' day. I want wine."

"Try that, and tell me what you think of it," continued Mr. Cripps, putting a bottle before him.

Franklin poured out a glass and tasted it, after which he made a wry face.

"Don't like it," he said. "It's worse than cherry brandy."

"Taste this," replied Cripps, giving him number two.

"Wherever have you been buying your wines, Cripps?" cried Franklin.

"Won't it do?"

"South African—no bouquet—no crust—no wing."

"Try again."

Franklin took up another glass, and essayed number three. He smacked his lips, his eye brightened, he drank.

"Ha!" he exclaimed, "that's something like. You can't fool me on wines. If a waiter had brought me those two first brands at a restaurant, I'd have made him acquainted with the business end of my boot. The last is wine, and no mistake."

"Franklin," answered Cripps, "I like you."

"Why?"

"You are a straightforward man. Those three wines are what I call my test of character. If I want to see what a man is made of, I put him to the test. Most men praise any wine I give them, for fear of offending me. They little think I am reckoning them up all the while. Many a man has wondered why I would not do business with him. It was because he could not stand my test."

"Well, that's hardly fair."

"Isn't it?"

"A man does not always like to abuse another man's wine, when he has got his legs under his mahogany; but I speak my mind, though it is not the way to get on in the world."

"It's the way to get on with me," replied Mr. Poppleton Cripps; who was in an excellent humour. When this was the case, he had a way of quoting poetry of his own composition, and asking his hearer where it came from.

"I shall take a pride in my cellar, when I marry and settle," remarked Franklin.

"Ah," said Cripps, "remember the lines—

> 'The spring of youth 's the carnival of life,
> And chilling winter enters with a wife.'

Who wrote that?" he added.

"Byron," replied the broker.

"No, sir. I'll ask you something else, suggested to me by the war rumours—

> 'Fight for a grateful country, lose a leg,
> Then die of glory, hang, or starve, or beg.'

Who's the author of those telling lines?"

"Pope, I should say."

"Wrong again. Once more—

> 'Death is busy, blithe are undertakers' firms,
> And merrily laughs the purveyor of worms.'"

"Ingoldsby."

"No. Who is the purveyor of worms? Why, the sexton, of course. Ha! ha! I thought I'd puzzle you. *I* wrote those couplets. You did not know I was a poet. Some day I'll show you a few of my compositions; but with regard to marrying. If you are in earnest, why not pay attention to Nellie. I will help you all I can, and at my death she will be well off.

"I should like nothing better, if I thought I could interest the young lady," replied Franklin.

"Sound her. Take her for a walk in the country. It is a nice stroll to the Lead Works through a pretty country I'll give you an order to go over them."

Thus encouraged, George Franklin resolved to put his scheme into execution without any further delay. Indeed time was pressing, he did not see any way out of his difficulties, and he would have to fly, whether Nellie accompanied him or not. At tea time he asked Miss Vine if she would be his guide to the Works. She was pleased to consent; he had to return to town that night, and she undertook to meet him at the station the next day at one o'clock. During the walk he would have an excellent opportunity of talking to her, and he was vain enough to believe that if he offered her his hand she would accept it, and go to the end of the world with him if he asked her. Nellie looked forward to this ramble with a great deal of interest, for she had already learnt to love Mr. Franklin, although she carefully concealed her real sentiments. She wished to learn more ot his character before she allowed him to know his power over her. Poor girl! She was much more in love with the handsome, gentlemanly rogue than she had any idea of. He had a good voice, and sang sentimental songs with wonderful pathos. Often had her little heart thrilled to its innermost chords as she listened to him. She started at his footstep; she turned warm and red at the sound of his voice; but her maiden innocence prevented her from even guessing that she was hopelessly in love.

It was a lovely summer morning, and the sweet smell of the new mown hay was wafted towards her as she stood in the lane near the station, waiting for the train to come in. She wore a muslin dress, and a provokingly pretty Leghorn shepherdess hat, trimmed with Marguerites and roses. On her arm was a small basket, which she had filled with cowslips, daisies, and buttercups, as she came along. She was a Watteau picture, framed in all the glory of the trees and the sunlight; the west wind kissed her rosy cheeks and fluttered her auburn curls as she waited, full of health and expectation; though she looked for the coming walk with an eagerness she could not account for, she was somewhat shy. It was the first time in her young and saint-like life that she had ever gone out alone with a man; she hoped, she thought, she almost believed that George Franklin was as good and pure as herself. She pictured him honest, diligent, noble-minded, and a distant worshipper hitherto of women. It pleased her to think that she was the first one of her sex that he had bowed down before, little dreaming that a score of women had bitter cause to curse the day they met him. Little did she guess that he had laid awake night after night to plot and plan how to get from his clients the bank notes he had in his pocket, the non-payment of which would in a few hours cause him to be posted as a defaulter. In fact, he had that day resolved not to go back to his office—he was even then a defaulter. This she had to learn. This was the worthless clay she loved. If she had known the man as he was, she would have flown from him as from a pestilence, and worn out the remainder of her life in weeping, rather than have listened to one word he had to say.

At length the train came in, and the broker seeing her in the lane hastened to join her. In a few set conventional phrases he thanked her for her kindness, praised the weather, and hoped they would enjoy the walk. Well-dressed, in rude health and excellent form, never had George Franklin appeared to more advantage. His looks, his words, his smiles led him to victory; and before they had gone a hundred yards towards the Works, Nellie Vine felt that she could give herself to him, if he asked her; for such a man she thought she could die. To him she was pretty and winsome, but he had seen women who had pleased him better. As a lever to get Mr. Poppleton Cripps' money, she was well enough; so he chatted gaily until he fancied it was time to throw off the mask a little.

"Do you like men of the world, Nellie?" he asked.

"I do not know," she replied; "for I have never met one."

"I am one."

"Really! Then I must, for I like you."

"Ah!" he exclaimed, "that is cold. Now, if you only loved me as I love you—do not start—the time has arrived when I must make you acquainted with the state of my heart. I loved you from the first moment I saw you, and the feeling has deepened into one of mad, passionate devotion. I cannot live without you. Excuse my abruptness, pardon my haste. I ask you, Nellie; I beg you to be my wife."

She cast down her eyes; he took her hand; it trembled in his; her emotion was very great. They were standing still, all alone in the shaded lane. The moments passed. She did not refuse him.

"I have spoken to your Guardian. He has given me leave to win you if I can. Let us go to London to-morrow and be married. Then we can go and bury ourselves somewhere in the country, no one knowing who we are. My love is selfish. I want you all to myself. Fly with me," he urged.

She looked up.

There was an expression of wonderment on her face. She did not quite understand this haste and secrecy. No doubt it was very romantic; but all her acts hitherto could bear the light of day.

"I love you," she replied. "It is useless for me to attempt to deny it, and I am willing to be your wife; but I can see no reason why we should not be made one in the sight of your friends and my friends."

"That will take time. It cannot be," he answered, breathing heavily.

"Why cannot it?"

"That is my secret."

"Oh! if we are to begin with a secret, I recall what I said," she cried.

"You cannot recall it."

"Yes, yes; I cannot unsay my words; you know that I

love you, and with me to love once is to love always; but I may not be the wife of a man who is afraid to bare his heart to me."

They had walked on again. She was plucking a flower petal from petal unconsciously He wore a scowl on his brow, and looked troubled. She had a God and a conscience. He had neither, and he was embarrassed, for he did not know how to deal with a girl of this sort. Strange to say, this man, who never before had been afraid of a woman, began to tremble before this girl of eighteen.

"I will trust you," he said, after a silence which weighed like a stone on both of them.

"If I am to love, I must be trusted, though I do not ask for your confidence," she replied.

"You shall know my secret, Nellie."

"Stop," she cried. "Something tells me it will be best I should not hear it."

"Then we must part."

"Yes, if you cannot proclaim me your wife before all men."

"No! Nothing but death shall part us, Nellie," he said, quickly. "I have found a pearl in you, and I am not going to give it up like this. I will tell you all, and throw myself on your mercy."

It had taken some time to say all this. They were close to the Works now, and they could see some little tanks in front of them, into which the molten lead was running from the furnaces.

In the immediate neighbourhood of the Works nothing grew. Its poisonous vapour killed all things; not even a dog, cat, or fowl lived where it was dry. Vegetation perished. Was not this typical of Franklin's love for her?

A dull, heavy atmosphere hung like a pall about the place, through which the molten lead in the tanks glowed like silver.

So occupied were both, that they scarcely noticed anything.

Franklin took a pocket-book from inside his coat and hastily opened it, showing a roll of bank notes, amounting to many thousands.

"You see this money," he ejaculated.

"Yes," she replied, simply.

He held it out, and let the wind flutter the notes.

"I have nearly £30,000 here. It's a small fortune. I have got this money by my heart's blood. I went for it," he continued.

"You did what?" she asked; not comprehending his meaning. "Is it not all yours?"

"No; it ought to be paid, and more too, in a few hours."

"Well; you will get the balance and pay it, will you not?"

"No, again. I have left the city never to return."

"What! you will not pay your debts?"

"I am a defaulter; but it is all for you."

"You offer me, *me*, other people's money; that which is not yours to give; stolen money!"

"Nellie! Miss Vine! Nellie!"

There was no answer.

"Nellie! do not look at me in that way!"

"Oh, my God," moaned the wretched girl; "help me, O Lord!"

She had sunk on her knees, her hands were clasped, her eyes, streaming with tears, were upturned to heaven. It was a sin that such a man should have crossed her path and taught her to love him; he had broken her heart.

"What have I done?" he asked.

"A defaulter!" she murmured.

"That is nothing. Lots of men can't settle. It's thought nothing of in the city. I'll pay so much in the pound, some day."

She shook her head.

If this was commercial morality, she would have none of it.

To her, he was a whitened sepulchre—fair without, but foul within. Never could she meet him, as a friend even, again; all must of necessity be at an end between them. Yet, for the sake of her love, and for his sake, it was her duty to try to save him from the pit he was digging for himself.

She rose to her feet, staggering beneath a weight of woe.

It was pitiable to see her agonized face; her heaving

bosom showed the agitation of her mind. She spoke with difficulty.

"It is not too late to save yourself," she exclaimed.

"How?" he queried.

"They do not know that you are a defaulter?"

"Not yet."

"Go and face your creditors; pay them what you can; ask for time."

"And be a beggar," he said, sarcastically.

"Yes; an honest beggar. You are young and strong, work your way up again."

"I hate work. You do not know the value of money."

"It is not yours!"

"By heaven! no one shall take it from me. Put aside this weakness, Nellie. With me you will be happy. I swear that I will live for you alone. With the notes I hold in my hand I am rich."

"A rich rogue."

"Upon my word, you are not complimentary."

"Go! Leave me! You have done me a great wrong. May heaven forgive you."

"A wrong—you!"

"Yes. I am only a poor simple-minded girl, but you have fallen like a blight on my young life."

"Nellie!"

"Away! I command you!" she exclaimed, drawing herself up to her full height, and regarding him with scorn.

How small, how utterly insignificant, the man felt then.

He laid his hand upon her shoulder. She threw him off, with an intense loathing in her glance.

"Do not touch me. It is pollution," she said, in freezing tones.

The jerk caused the pocket book to fall from his hand, and the wind caught the packet of notes.

A sudden eddying, whirling gust bore them towards a tank of boiling, hissing, seething lead, to which the pair had, unawares, advanced perilously near.

A moment more and the notes fell in.

George Franklin uttered a sharp, wild cry. The bank

notes were fluttering in the lead. Soon the molten mass would engulf and destroy them.

Nellie Vine's distress had not moved him.

The loss of his money made him a madman.

"Good God!" he screamed, tottering like a drunken coward, "I am ruined! My money! My money! Give me back my money!"

Nellie moved away suddenly. He did not know she was gone until he heard the gentle rustling of her muslin gown.

She went straight towards the boiling lead. A haze covered it, but through the haze could be seen the notes.

The foreman came out of his house.

He instantly recognised the young mistress, and an awful fear seized him, for he thought that she did not see where she was going.

"Take care, Miss," he shouted.

Nellie, paying no heed, walked on.

"Look out, Miss; you'll be into the lead," continued the foreman.

She did not slacken her speed, nor so much as turn her head.

George Franklin watched her as if she had been a ghost.

What was she going to do? It was more than he could fathom. His shallow mind knew nothing of self-sacrifice; he was ignorant of woman's devotion. Incapable of noble impulses himself, he could not realize such a thing in another.

She reached the brink.

The packet of notes was partially under the surface. Stretching out her hand, Nellie Vine plunged it into the tank and drew out the money. She had saved the notes from destruction—but at what a cost!

Shivering from head to foot, suppressing with difficulty a cry of suffering which came to her lips through excruciating pain, she retraced her steps.

When she reached George Franklin, she was as white as the paper the notes were printed upon.

"There is your money, Mr. Franklin," she exclaimed.

Eagerly he clutched the precious wealth.

o

"How can I thank you?" he said. "But you are hurt—your hand!"

He paused, horror stricken. She was burned to the bone. That fair right hand was withered.

Never would she be able to use it again.

"Farewell," she murmured, faintly. "Pay your debts. Let no man say a word against your honour. Farewell, for ever."

She took a step forward, as if she would go home; but a soul-harrowing, pent-up cry of agony broke from her, and she fell on her face insensible.

George Franklin took one look at her, and then ran from the spot like one possessed, and, as he ran, her words rang in his ears—

"Farewell. Let no man say a word against your honour. Farewell—for ever."

But after going some distance he halted, and was constrained to return to the fatal spot. He was half maddened; he knew not what he did. It was all too horrible. When he reached the Mills there was no one about. Nellie Vine had been taken away.

In a fit of despair, which he could not check, he gazed curiously at the molten lead, which still poured in a hissing stream from the furnace.

"I will do it, I must do it!" he cried, with a maniacal laugh.

The next moment he threw himself headlong into the boiling metal, and as the mass cooled off, it clung to his lifeless body.

He had made for himself a leaden coffin.

When the dreadful end of the defaulter was made known, even those whom he had robbed could not repress a shudder of pity at his awful though self-inflicted fate.

THE END.

www.ingramcontent.com/pod-product-compliance
Lightning Source LLC
Chambersburg PA
CBHW020901230426
43666CB00008B/1267